"Alongside a brilliant mind, she demonstrates a heart of gold. Dr. Madeleine's challenging journey from Mollendo, Peru, to the U.S. exemplifies much more than a quest for higher education. Far from the comforting environment of her family and close friends in Peru, Madeleine forged a path of distinction rooted in her trademark bravery, grit and resilience.

Earning her positioning as a nationally renowned scientist, Madeleine realized her remarkable gift of solving real-world problems. Now, she offers her ingenuity and academic frameworks to you through a convenient, understandable, and turnkey approach.

I have known Madeleine for many years. I admire her not only for her distinguished knowledge, but also for her integrity and honesty. This lived experience of strong mind and character emanate throughout this breakthrough read. Drawing on her rigorous education as a Ph.D. in Sociology (Demography and Statistics) and her experience across both private and public sectors, Madeleine presents opportunities to eradicate the most damaging business problems with clarity and confidence.

Equally compelling, Madeleine empowers individuals and enterprises from all backgrounds to become transformation doers, not just transformation evangelists. Magnificently, The SEAM Framework is delivered with a brilliant mind and a heart of gold. Truly Madeleine."

—**MARK L. MADRID**, Honorary Colonel, United States Army, Jefferson Award honoree

---

"Dr. Madeleine Wallace's beautiful journey from the nostalgic streets of Peru to the forefront of digital transformation make for an inspiring and practical guide for leaders today. Through real-life examples and the innovative SEAM framework, this book brilliantly illuminates the path to navigating technological change in business and life. A tribute to resilience, adaptability, and the human spirit, it's more than a guide—it's an invitation to embrace change as the greatest opportunity for growth."

—**LILI GIL VALLETTA**, Award-winning entrepreneur, Chief Executive Officer Culture+ Group, Corporate Board Director and TV Business Commentator

"This book is a game changer! In just 4 steps, it masterfully guides organizations through a profound transformation journey. Wallace's expertise shines through, offering practical strategies that empower teams and drive success. An indispensable guide for any leader seeking to navigate the complex landscape of organizational change."

—STACI LATOISON, Dream Big Ventures Founder and CEO

"Kudos to Dr Madeleine Wallace for penning The SEAM Framework. Dr Wallace elegantly and with great clarity shows the reader a roadmap with easy-to-use tools that will help immensely in addressing the plethora of customer needs in this highly competitive market."

—SANJIV CHOPRA, MBBS MACP FRCP, Professor of Medicine, Harvard Medical School, Renowned Inspirational Keynote Speaker

---

"I firmly believe that frameworks play a vital role in guiding businesses and organizations toward sustainable growth. 'THE SEAM FRAMEWORK' appears to offer valuable insights and practical toolkits that can empower readers and companies to navigate the ever-changing landscape of customer requirements and build robust infrastructures. I hope that those who delve into this book find it to be a valuable resource in their journey toward success."

—CLAUDIA ROMO EDELMAN, Founder & CEO, We Are All Human Foundation

THE
SEAM
FRAMEWORK

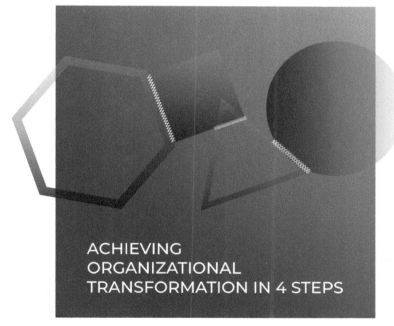

ACHIEVING
ORGANIZATIONAL
TRANSFORMATION IN 4 STEPS

Madeleine F. Wallace, PhD

The SEAM FRAMEWORK
ACHIEVING ORGANIZATIONAL TRANSFORMATION IN 4 STEPS

For more information contact:

Email: mfw@madeleinewallace.com
www.madeleinewallace.com

Cover Design and Layout by Fig Factor Media LLC
Printed in the United States of America

ISBN: 978-1-959989-61-5
Library of Congress Control Number: 2023916749

TABLE OF CONTENTS

FOREWORD

Change is a constant companion in the journey of life and business. It resonates with all of us, often pushing us out of our comfort zones, and yet it remains an exciting opportunity to grow and evolve. The following pages tell a story of change, adapting to new realities, resilience, and transformation.

Dr. Madeleine Wallace moves from the nostalgic memories of Mollendo, Peru, where typewriters were once the future, to the bustling streets of Arequipa, intertwining personal stories with the ever-shifting landscape of technology. The tale of a family-run school uprooted by the advent of computers is a poignant reminder of how change can be both unforgiving and empowering.

The necessary transition from one form of technology to another is more than a technological evolution; it's a metaphor for the adaptability required in modern business. And it's called transformation. Whether it's a cleaning service pondering the path to automation or a health clinic considering how to utilize electronic health records (EHR) systems, the question is the same: How can one adapt and thrive in a world defined by continuous change?

This book introduces you to the concept of Digital Transformation through the lens of the SEAM framework - Snapshot, Envision, Act, and Measure. It's a holistic and practical guide, grounded in real-world examples and simulated stories, illustrating how small businesses and organizations can navigate the complex terrain of technological advancement.

Growing a career in technology leadership, I quickly learned that change happens by us, with us, or to us. As my business grew into a large enterprise, it would have been ideal to have SEAM help navigate the acceleration of my business through a technological lens. As an entrepreneur of technology, I can now use this essential framework to build my business. It's a handbook for those who see change not as a threat but as an invitation to innovate.

As you explore these pages, you will discover how the journey to digital transformation is not merely about adopting new technologies but about reshaping entire organizations, cultures, and mindsets. You'll find guidance, inspiration, and the tools to embark on this ever-evolving journey.

Your guide on this voyage is Dr. Wallace's wealth of experience, insights, and intimate connection to the subject matter, imbuing these pages with authenticity and wisdom. It will not only bring a sound foundation for digital transformation to your business but also ask the inspiring question: If she can do it, why can't you?

Guillermo Diaz, Jr
Founder / CEO Conectado Inc.
Fomer CIO, Cisco Systems

DEDICATION

I dedicate this book to my amazing family …

To the loving memory of my mother, whose extraordinary legacy continues to shape every aspect of my life. She was a visionary who fearlessly advocated for women's rights and stood firm in her beliefs and values. Authenticity was her essence, and she was never one to follow the crowd. Her unwavering support and example have molded me into the dedicated professional I am today. She actively encouraged, mentored, and opened doors for her students to pursue non-traditional roles and to seek advancements in the workplace. She understood the multifaceted responsibilities of women and adjusted her teaching schedule to accommodate her female students in balancing their various commitments. Through her, I learned the true meaning of empowering and championing the endeavors of other women through tangible actions, not mere words.

To my father, whose lifelong commitment to education has indelibly impacted countless individuals spanning different generations. He wholeheartedly embraces the notion that every person learns in unique ways, and he tirelessly developed various techniques to cater to diverse learning styles. He is a stalwart advocate for instilling core values from an early age and recognizing their profound influence on character and personal growth. His wisdom and unwavering passion for teaching ignited my desire to share knowledge and inspire the growth of others.

To my sister Rosemarie, a compassionate and dedicated doctor who selflessly serves her patients and remains committed to improve her community. She exemplifies leadership at its core, leading with unwavering integrity and consistently prioritizing the well-being of others. From her, I learned the immeasurable value of selfless service and the fulfillment that comes from giving without expecting anything in return.

To my sister Eveline, a fearless serial entrepreneur who has demonstrated the power of belief in self and the courage to pursue dreams relentlessly. She has taught me the importance of realism, emphasizing that no task is too small or insignificant. Her willingness to roll up her sleeves has been instrumental in shaping my approach to work.

I dedicate this book to them, who are my love and inspiration.

ACKNOWLEDGMENTS

The writing of this book has been an incredible journey. Unlike my previous academic writing experiences where journal formats dictated clear boundaries, this book pushed me to present concepts in a story-telling format, ensuring practical application rather than mere theoretical concepts. It has further strengthened my ability to bridge the gap between theoretical business models and real-life applications.

Throughout this journey, there were weeks when my creative juices flowed abundantly, and excitement fueled my progress. However, there also were challenging times when I needed to step back and take a break from writing. During these moments of both inspiration and struggle, I owe my deepest gratitude to the individuals who supported and encouraged me.

I want to express my heartfelt appreciation to my dear friend, Yaeli Merenfeld, who generously took time to lend an ear to my preliminary ideas about the book. She was excited about the Snapshot, Envision, Act and Measure (SEAM) model because of its practical applications to all businesses and organizations. Beyond that, she taught me to appreciate the art of making artisanal bread—to savor the aroma and texture and to find inspiration in the process. Touring her facility was a truly inspiring experience, and I felt as though the bread itself was whispering messages to me. I am thankful for Yaeli's commitment to read my entire book, including the figures. She was very pleased to see the templates for SEAM users.

I am also deeply grateful to Maria Fernanda Reyes. Her unwavering confidence in my work and trust in its value for business have been invaluable. It was Maria Fernanda who encouraged me to take the critical step of building a community of followers for my SEAM framework even before its release. Her support led to a presentation at the Women Entrepreneur Forum DC: Women Entrepreneurs Forum | Beyond 2023: A New Era of Innovation and Leadership.

I'd like to thank the entire Fig Factor Media team for their very thoughtful review and critical assistance.

Last, but certainly not least, I extend my deepest gratitude to Stephen, my spouse. He is not just my life partner but also my steadfast supporter, my tireless cheerleader, and my most cherished confidant. His unwavering patience was constant as I carried my laptop to every conceivable place we went—vacations and international travels included. Through his eyes, I am endowed with brilliance and an unrelenting spirit that can surmount any challenge. His faith in the success of the businesses I created has been both humbling and empowering.

INTRODUCTION

Why SEAM?

My inspiration for writing this book wasn't just another academic pursuit or a casual hobby. Instead, it was a deeply personal journey, sparked by the painful memory of watching my parents' vocational school shutter its doors as they struggled to transition from typewriters to the rapidly evolving world of computers.

The stories shared by my colleagues, the struggles of my small and large business clients, and their challenges, defeats, and victories are threads woven into the fabric of this book. It's clear that small businesses face unique challenges that require specialized guidance because, unlike larger corporations, they often lack substantial resources and dedicated information technology (IT) department to navigate the complexities of digital transformation. This is precisely where I step in to bridge the gap. With a deep understanding of the particular needs and constraints of small businesses and organizations, I provide tailored guidance to launch them on their way to greater success.

SEAM is an acronym for four steps of transformation: Snapshot, Envision, Act, and Measure. Over twenty years, I've applied this framework extensively to assist federal agencies, businesses, academia, foundations, and organizations in evaluating the results of their various programs, policies, and interventions. I've employed it to drive change at all levels—systemic, organizational, and individual. The approach may vary, depending on who we are trying to transform, but the framework applies in all situations.

When using SEAM, it is essential to understand who or what we are trying to transform. Are we overhauling an entire system, reforming an organization, or changing individual behaviors? In the context of this book, I primarily focus on how to steer the whole organization into the digital era. I aim to ensure they not just adapt, but flourish within the evolving digital landscape by leveraging technology, data, and digital capabilities to their maximum potential.

SEAM is a flexible framework designed to be adaptable and accessible to all—whether you are a solopreneur trying to navigate digital transformation alone, a small team working tirelessly to update your business, or an organization employing the services of a con-sultant. This book is your companion, a guiding light to navigate you to a seamless digital transformation.

I am a visual person, so I have included templates to apply what you've learned and to visualize change in your organization. These templates will help you internalize the outlined concepts and strategies and create unique action plans for your business or organization based on applying the SEAM framework. This engaging approach serves as a crucial bridge between abstract understanding and concrete execution and provides an immersive reading experience. To continue learning beyond the last chapter, I invite you to visit my website at madeleinewallace.com. There, you'll find additional resources, updates, and a vibrant community of like-minded individuals to support you in your organizational transformation. SEAM is not just a source of information; it's an invitation to embark on an exciting, endless journey of personal and professional development.

Bridging Sectors

Over the years, I have had the privilege of serving as a consultant and advisor, evaluating the effectiveness of large programs, initiatives, and efforts for esteemed federal agencies such as the National Institutes of Health (NIH) and the National Science Foundation (NSF). In this capacity, my role spanned a diverse range of fields, encompassing science, technology, engineering, and math (STEM), biomedical training, and translational research. Each evaluation represented a profound exploration into the intricacies of the respective field, addressing its distinctive challenges, identifying opportunities, and discovering the levers of change capable of driving it to new heights. United by a common commitment to advancing science, working with federal agencies has profoundly influenced my perspective in the field of innovation. This has equipped me with a distinct skillset to bridge interdisciplinary gaps, transcending traditional boundaries.

Building on a successful track record in corporate America overseeing large-scale projects and a distinguished career in government as the director of evaluation and performance for the NIH, I founded and currently lead Windrose Vision, a strategy and research consulting company. For more than ten years, we have been helping organizations turn ideas into strategic actions by unlocking the power of data-driven, evidence-based approaches to their respective markets including industries, foundations, nonprofits, and the federal government.

With SEAM, I present a unique approach using my proficiency and expertise in performance-based management and program evaluation. These disciplines demand meticulous scrutiny, a deep understanding of complex systems, and a commitment to fostering a culture of continuous improvement and accountability.

As you read this book, you'll benefit from my multi-faceted background, which underpins the practical and effective approach I bring to the business consulting domain. The diversity of insight fuels SEAM and its rigorous, methodical approach to understanding problems and identifying solutions. This is a critical distinction that sets the framework apart—it is not tied to a specific industry or technology but is a versatile and adaptable framework to guide your efforts in any field. Captured within the pages of this book, SEAM ensures that no matter your industry, the size of your business, or the challenges you face, you will find directly applicable guidance and strategies to streamline your journey to digital transformation.

All the figures and blank templates are available in appendix 1 at the end of the book.

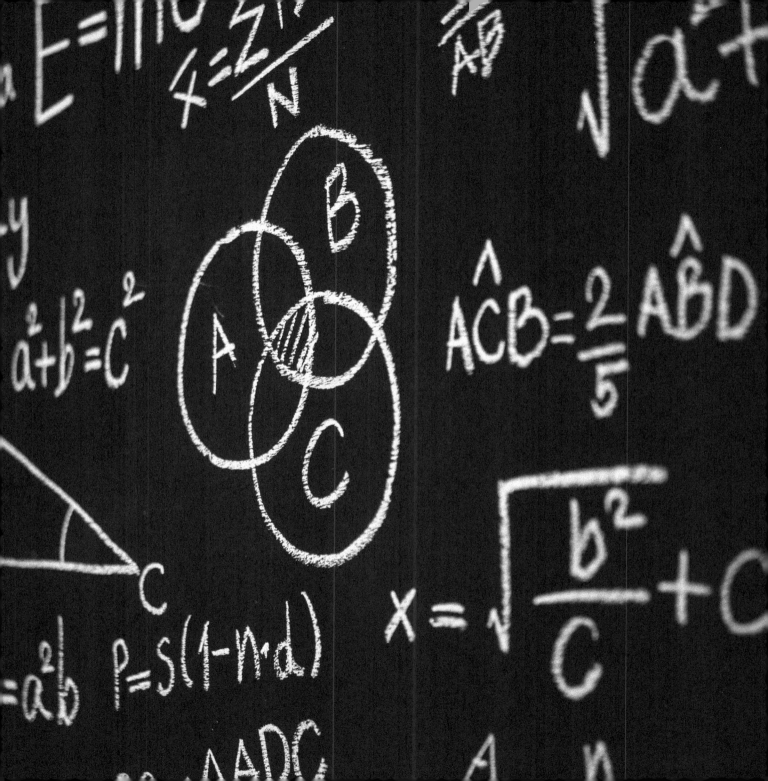

Chapter 1
Responding to Fast and Furious Change

"The greatest danger in times of turbulence is not the turbulence—it is to act with yesterday's logic."

Peter Drucker

Change is an absolute shared human experience at work and in life. And so many times, how we react to those changes defines our happiness, our fortunes, and our future.

I grew up in Peru in the small town of Mollendo, a casual, relaxed coastal town with beautiful beaches off the Pacific Ocean. My parents earned a comfortable living operating a vocational school there. We trained administrative assistants with office and bookkeeping skills to prepare them for work in small and large businesses. My mother taught shorthand and typing, and my father taught business administration. They kept up with the latest trends and invested in the school to prepare for the future. One of them was the purchase of electric typewriters. Things went well for years until a new threat to the school's business model quickly emerged: computers.

Suddenly, electric typewriters, my family's investment for the future, became obsolete. People wanted to learn how to use a computer and type into a word processing program, not onto paper. Then the government began offering free computer classes to the people of Mollendo. While this was a boon to our town, we could not compete. It decimated our family business.

We moved to Arequipa, Peru, a larger city close to Mollendo. My parents found work in a large vocational school that offered business courses, including computers. They taught students the principles of business administration. The role was completely new for them, and the move to the larger city was difficult for all of us. There were cultural differences between laid-back Mollendo and bustling Arequipa, which had the charm, traditions, and colder weather of an inland Spanish colonial city. My parents were unknown in Arequipa, while in Mollendo, they were well known and respected. Pivoting from an entrepreneur to an employee was particularly difficult for them.

My story illustrates how unexpected change can shake you from your comfort zone and alter your life forever. However, it also shows how you can successfully take your expertise, like my parents did with their teaching, and apply it to a new setting. We can easily become victims of change if we aren't flexible and always looking ahead to see what is on the horizon.

DIGITAL TRANSFORMATION: THE EVER-EVOLVING JOURNEY IN A SHIFTING TECHNOLOGICAL LANDSCAPE

When computers swooped in to replace electric typewriters at my parents' vocational school, my parents faced a critical juncture. They could either maintain the status quo with their typewriters, thereby risking obsolescence or pivot their business strategy to fully embrace the new computer-based paradigm.

Today's small businesses and organizations often confront similar crossroads that require critical strategic decisions about their future direction. As the founder and CEO of Windrose Vision, a strategy and consulting firm, I've witnessed firsthand the struggles my clients face as they strive to remain competitive amid swiftly evolving digital technologies and dynamic consumer behaviors.
Here are four examples:

• **A Local Cleaning Service.**
The business has traditionally been suc-

cessful based on word-of-mouth recommendations and the quality of their service. However, they must now consider a path to digital transformation. Should they create a website to increase visibility? Adopt technology by integrating an online booking and payment system? Or should they undergo a complete transformation, adapting the Internet of Things (IoT) devices for efficient cleaning, a customer service chatbot, or even an app that allows real-time tracking of the cleaning progress?

• A Small Construction Firm.

A company that once relied heavily on manual processes and face-to-face communications now must consider emerging digital technology solutions in their industry. The firm could adopt an advanced project management software to streamline operations or leverage 3D modeling software to enhance their construction planning process. They also might fully transform their operations by integrating artificial intelligence (AI) predictive analytics for risk management and utilizing drones and IoT for real-time site monitoring.

Organizations also face critical decisions about digital technology, as shown in these examples.

• A Nonprofit Organization.

An organization that delivers in-person training programs for high schoolers pursuing STEM careers faces a proliferation of online learning platforms and mobile technologies. It needs to decide how to recruit and engage high schoolers. Should it set up an e-learning platform or develop a mobile app? Or should it transform its delivery model entirely to online courses, webinars, and virtual mentoring, potentially reaching a global audience?

• A Health Clinic.

As digital technologies in healthcare have enhanced patient care and operational efficiency, the health clinic must consider implementing an electronic health records (EHR) system. Doing so would digitize patient data and administrative processes, improve data accessibility, reduce paperwork, and enhance coordination among healthcare providers. They also must consider adopting telemedicine capabilities, including remote consultations, virtual visits, and remote patient monitoring to improve access to healthcare services.

These examples reveal the ongoing challenges and opportunities businesses and organizations encounter in today's dynamic environment. But what is digital transformation? It is not one thing in particular but a perpetual journey within this continuum with three stages of development. These stages are not always linear, and organizations might move back and forth between them or even be in different stages simultaneously in different parts of the organization. (Rogers, D. L. 2016)

THREE STAGES OF DIGITAL TRANSFORMATION

If my parents had embraced technology, their three stages of technological transformation would have looked like this.

THE INITIAL STAGE: This stage marks the initial response to technology, or in my parent's case, the advent of computers. My parents would understand the growing importance of computer skills and make a strategic choice to integrate them into their curriculum. They would swap typewriters for computers and educate their students on the novel tools. The fundamental nature of their business would remain the same—providing vocational train-ing—but they would update the methods to meet current demands. Their major challenge, however, would lie in distinguishing their offerings from the free government classes.

THE INTERMEDIATE STAGE: Here, the business or organization builds upon its adoption of technology. My parents would adapt their business model to align with the new reality. In addition to integrating computers into the curriculum, they would modify their course offerings to provide more specialized and advanced training in advanced software, graphic design, or programming. By doing so, they could maintain their competitiveness and continue to deliver value despite the emergence of freely available classes.

THE TRANSFORMATION STAGE: In this stage, businesses may embrace an entirely new business model. My parents could radically shift their local vocational school into an international online education platform, offering a broad spectrum of computer courses. By leveraging online learning technologies, they could extend their reach to a broader audience and offer students the convenience of learning at their own pace, from anywhere. They also could collaborate with businesses to provide tailor-made training programs, serving as a conduit between education and industry. Such an all-encompassing digital transformation would surely keep them competitive amid evolving circumstances.

In today's practices, businesses or organizations can completely overhaul their culture, structure, and operations if they embrace a digital-first mindset and prioritize agility, innovation, and customer-centricity. In this context, digital transformation becomes a holistic approach to reshaping the organization to thrive in the rapidly evolving digital landscape.

By embracing digital technology, organizations and businesses become flexible enough to navigate between different areas of concern, adapting to specific needs and circumstances. For example, an organization might initially embark on a radical transformation that drives significant shifts in its operations. Later, they might pivot and make incremental improvements based on customer feedback or changing requirements. Alternatively, a company might start with modest changes to test the waters and later embrace more profound transformations as their digital capabilities evolve.

We must acknowledge that the decision to embark on the transformation journey can be influenced by a multitude of factors, including:

- Access to capital
- Risk tolerance
- Market dynamics
- Industry standards
- People and business networks
- Available technology
- Access to information
- Digital maturity
- Organization size
- Team skill set

This is just a short list of critical factors that must be considered when making informed decisions and successfully navigating the path to digital transformation.

Let's keep in mind that the specific journey of every organization or business depends on its unique circumstances and strategic vision. During my parents' time, information about the rapidly evolving technological landscape

was scarce or virtually non-existent. Consequently, they needed help to develop a distinct offering to differentiate themselves from the free government classes. They could not secure funds for essential computer equipment and could not allocate resources to train their staff in the new teaching methods required for the digital transition. Sadly, they saw no other option than to close their business. SEAM could have helped them!

SEAM FOR DIGITAL TRANSFORMATION

SEAM, as shown in Figure 1.1, is a robust and highly effective framework that empowers small businesses and organizations to embark on their digital transformation journey with confidence and clarity.

SEAM is adaptable. Users can implement the framework at any stage, whether they are just starting their transformation journey, in the middle of it, or in the throes of a complete transformation of their organization. SEAM allows businesses and organizations to leverage its benefits anywhere within the transformational process.

Fig. 1.1. Four-Step SEAM Framework

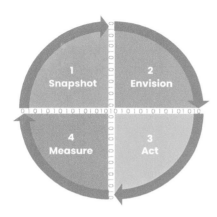

SEAM champions digital transformation efforts in four critical organizational outcomes: financial, customer, partner, and people. SEAM guides the user in formulating these outcomes and connecting them to various aspects of digital transformation, such as automation, digitization, digitalization, data analytics, enhanced customer experiences, the development of innovative business models, and the initiation of cultural change. (Siebel 2019) (Westerman, Bonnet, and McAfee 2014) I have made these connections explicit so you can envision the tangible benefits of digital transformation for your business.

As an experienced developer of training materials for diverse audiences in the private, public, academia, and nonprofit sectors, I have included a variety of fillable templates in each step of the SEAM framework. Every template facilitates critical thinking, decision-making, and execution of your digital transformation plan. Think of this book as a guide and working document to use in your digital transformation journey. It will help you convert your ideas into actionable steps, making the path to digital transformation more tangible and manageable.

To demonstrate the application of SEAM, let's focus on one specific, fictional business called Mora's Bakery, a small producer of artisan bread products. The business is fictitious, but the information and character of it are intricately woven from various aspects of my diverse projects. I aim to explain the abstract concepts behind SEAM by zeroing in on this singular yet comprehensive example. Through the experience of the fictional owner of the bakery, a lady named Mora, we will journey through the practicality and applicability of the model and discover how the framework addresses specific problems, providing a clear demonstration of its functionality within a real-world setting. This focused narrative will inspire and equip you to use the SEAM framework to tackle your own digital transformation challenges. Mora's Bakery is an accessible, relevant, and impactful example of how to use SEAM for your purposes.

ENTREPRENEURIAL SPIRIT: BURNING DESIRE TO MAKE AN IMPACT

The story of my parents does not end with the closing of their vocational school. Their entrepreneurial spirit was like an unceasing fire. Even when we moved to Arequipa, where they became employees rather than proprietors, the essence of their entrepreneurship never faded.

Every Saturday, they pivoted from their 9-to-5 jobs and became mentors for remedial middle school and high school students. Their efforts were not for monetary gain. They responded to a fundamental calling, a deeply rooted desire to contribute to society in the most profound way they knew how—through education.

They understood, perhaps better than anyone, that entrepreneurship isn't defined merely by owning a business. It's a mindset, a commitment, and a burning desire to make an impact. It's about paving your own path, not for the promise of financial returns, but for the gratification that stems from realizing your unique vision.

The relentless pursuit of their passion, even in the face of adversity, is a lesson I carry with me to this day. It's a lesson that resonates with anyone who finds joy in their work and perceives their business as not just a means to an end but an end in itself.

So, if you are reading these words and find your heart skipping a beat and your mind wandering back to your own business, passion, and determination to make a difference, know that you are not alone. You are part of a grand legacy of entrepreneurs defined not by wealth or success but by resilience, passion, and the insatiable desire to contribute to the world in a unique way. Just like my parents did every Saturday in their small classroom, we can shape the minds of the next generation, one lesson at a time.

SEAM is a conduit to focus and channel that entrepreneurial energy into a new way of looking at your business or organization. I have based it upon one of the staples I've used in my world—the logic model. SEAM employs the logic model, but I've adapted it in a way that will provide a strategy for even the most challenging digital transformation. Before we dive into SEAM, we must first learn a little about its foundation.

Are you ready to take the first step in showing your business the way to digital transformation? Let's go

All the figures and blank templates are available in appendix 1 at the end of the book.

Chapter 2

The Logic Model

"Logic is the technique by which
we add conviction to truth."

Jean de La Bruyère

The logic model is a widely used tool in the program evaluation field and the inspiration behind the SEAM framework for planning, executing, monitoring, and evaluating digital transformation efforts. Logic models have successfully helped organizations bring strategies, programs, projects, and initiatives to fruition. They are useful in a variety of fields (e.g., health, education, change management) in diverse settings (e.g., hospitals, universities, schools, businesses) and at different levels (e.g., individuals, families, schools, states, and nationwide.) (Knowlton and Phillips 2013)

The logic model is timeless, limitless, and so versatile that it can be applied to help a baker make better cupcakes or streamline Fortune 500 companies' IT operations. At Windrose Vision, the logic model is the start of any projects for businesses, nonprofits, government agencies, academia, and foundations.

WHAT IS A LOGIC MODEL?

Whenever you plan to do something with intention, the logic model illustrates the route to reach your goal. For example, the C-Suite may use a logic model to restructure, while

HR uses it to create a diversity, equity, and inclusion (DEI) initiative. The marketing department can apply a logic model to outline a social media campaign. Meanwhile, at a nearby university, professors huddled over a logic model to create a STEM program targeting first-generation college students.

I like to think of the logic model as a visual interpretation of a project, not unlike the visualization of DNA within the human body. As you may know (or remember from biology class), DNA stores the unique genetic information of an organism's cell. Similarly, a project's logic model is an essential part of planning, executing, and understanding a project. The code within the DNA provides directions on making proteins that are vital for growth, development, and overall health. Likewise, the logic model shows how specific steps are involved for the operation to reach its goals. Just as we never see DNA itself (except through a microscope), clients or customers may never know the path outlined in a logic model to reach an outcome. However, they will undoubtedly enjoy the benefits of a model!

In short, the logic model can distill the complexity of its subject into a graphic interpretation. In this way, it gives organizations a 20,000-foot view of their operations and a fresh viewpoint to its users. Gantt charts, process flows, and roadmaps share some similarities with logic models in that they are all visual tools for planning and management; however, they serve different purposes and focus on different aspects of projects or initiatives. Gantt charts deal with project scheduling, process flows illustrate workflows or processes, and roadmaps outline strategic plans. Logic models represent the relationships between program components and their expected outcomes.

COMPONENTS OF THE LOGIC MODEL

The components within the logic model function in a relationship. These components include inputs, activities, outputs, outcomes, and impact. Let's use a fictional example of launching a podcast to examine how a logic model can be used to illustrate a project and the relationship between all its components.

Noelle is a business coach who wants to launch a podcast with two goals in mind. First, she wants to raise awareness of the latest managerial techniques/skills for first-time

managers overseeing employees in a hybrid role (online and on-site). Second, and perhaps most importantly, she wants to boost her business coaching service. She hopes that listeners of her podcast will see her as a subject matter expert in business management and contact her for business coaching to become a better manager.

To prepare for the launch of her podcast, Noelle has taken voice training and performs weekly vocal exercises to improve her pitch, breathing, and enunciation. She researched the podcast market and found that first-time managers from the millennial generation overseeing employees in a hybrid role do not have a podcast that currently resonates with them. Noelle assumes that first-time managers will be hungry for the information they need to rise up the company ladder and will eagerly tune into the podcast. She plans to focus on one management technique for fifteen minutes for each podcast.

Figure 2.1 shows what Noelle's logic model might look like.

Fig 2.1. Noelle's Logic Model for the Podcast

INPUTS	ACTIVITIES	OUTPUTS	OUTCOMES			IMPACT
			Short-term (1 month)	**Intermediate (6 months)**	**Long-Term (1 year)**	
-Equipment -Software -Books and articles -Subscribers -Advertisers -Master Certified Coach (MCC) by the International Coaching Federation (ICF) -MBA with a concentration in Organizational Leadership and Change Management	**Four Phases:** **1. Plan** -Research existing podcasts that also provide managerial advice and target new managers. -Identify the unique selling proposition of this podcast compared to the competition. -Select podcast name, format (interview, solo/monologue, panel, etc.), length (15, 30, 60 minutes), frequency (daily, weekly, monthly). -Select and set up recording equipment, editing software, and space to produce the podcast. -Select a platform that does hosting and distribution of content to Apple, Google, etc. **2. Produce** -Record and edit content for at least five episodes. -Add advertising. -Add intro and outro, and invite to subscribe to both podcast and blog. **3. Promotion and engagement with listeners** -Promote the date of the podcast launch. -Create an audiogram from the first t episode and post it on Instagram. -Pick a quote from the first episode and post it on Linkedin. -Create and promote a blog to go with each episode. Blog Call To Action is to answer a question about a management technique and/or contact Noelle for coaching. -Create a website for the podcast. **4. Launch** -Prepare and upload the episodes to hosting and distribution platforms. -Monitor listenership.	**1. Plan** a weekly 15-minute solo/monologue **2. Produce** all activities completed **3. Promotion** all activities completed **4. Launch and Monitor** Number of unique listeners per episode -Number of followers per episode -Average percentage listened per episode -Number of subscribers to the blog -Days where the blog gains the biggest audience -Number of answers to a "prompt question" that Noelle will put in the blog positive -Audience demographics	**For the Listeners:** -10% of comments address the question of the blog and indicate that the commenters had prior knowledge of the management technique discussed in the podcast. **For the Coach:** -5% monthly increase in the audience for the podcast.	**For the Listeners:** -25% of comments address the question of the blog and indicate that the commenters used a management technique at work that they learned from the podcast. -5% of blog readers or podcast subscribers inquire about Noelle's coaching services. **For the Coach:** -Get first coaching client. One of the blog readers or podcast subscribers hire Noelle for coaching services.	**For the Listeners:** -2% of comments credit the podcast for directly contributing to a promotion or success at work. **For the Coach:** -15% of blog readers or podcast subscribers inquire about Noelle's coaching services. -Grow coaching services to five clients -Book two speaking opportunities within the next year	**For the Listeners:** -Rise to their highest desired level of management may be partially attributed to the excellent skills learned during coaching. **For the Coach:** -Become an international subject matter expert to newly minted young managers -Build a sustainable business with managerial coaching services

As shown in the example:

INPUTS: Encompasses the resources to reach the desired outcome. For Noelle, this includes the technology necessary to create a podcast, as well as everything she needs to research and plan it. The subscribers and advertisers also are essential inputs that Noelle will need to cultivate if the podcast is to succeed.

ACTIVITIES: Are actions taken to achieve outputs and outcomes. In this example, activities occur in four phases: plan, produce, promote, and launch.

OUTPUT: Are qualitative and quantifiable results from the activities. In this example, they present as measurable items, such as the number of listeners who perform specific actions.

OUTCOMES: Are the actual results or consequences that arise from the effort to achieve a goal. They are specific, measurable, and can be positive or negative. Outcomes occur progressively and are expressed as short-term, intermediate, and long-term outcomes. In our example, you can see that Noelle needs to collect data to determine whether she is meeting her outcomes. Whenever possible, the numbers you set for your outcomes should be based on best practices and what is standard in your industry for organizations of similar size.

Goals and outcomes are related concepts but have distinct differences in their definitions and applications. Goals represent the desired future state or objectives that individuals, teams, organizations, or businesses strive to achieve, while outcomes are the actual results or consequences that occur because of those efforts. Outcomes are usually influenced by a range of uncontrollable factors, including circumstances external to the goal creators, market conditions, technological advancements, natural and environmental conditions, as well as social and cultural factors. (Mertens and Wilson 2018) (Gothelf and Seiden 2017) Outcomes can be used to evaluate the effectiveness of actions, strategies, or interventions, but may not always align with intended goals due to unforeseen circumstances or changes in the environment. For example, a goal might be to bake a delicious loaf of bread, but the outcome may be an undercooked loaf because there was a power failure during baking.

IMPACT: Is the effect of the achieved outcome. Outcomes can be measured, but it is hard to measure impact because it implies a broader, overall change within a community, society, organization, or academia. Making an impact involves creating sustainable, long-term changes.

In Noelle's case, she may never know if she has had the desired impact shown in the last column of her logic model on her listeners unless they contact her and let her know they have become CEOs because of her podcast. She could try to gather the information through a survey in her blog. If her coaching business starts to gain traction among younger managers who share their experiences on the blog, she would have some insights into the podcast's influence on its listeners.

Using the logic model exposes the DNA of the podcast itself. In detail, you can see the materials and activities needed for success and how the podcast can make a lasting impression on a target audience of managerial millennials. This is the logic model in action and the basis for my SEAM framework, which we will learn more about in the coming chapters.

THEORY-DRIVEN CHANGE MODELS

Another type of model, which is a close cousin of the logic model, is the Theory of Change (ToC) model. The big difference between the two models is that the logic model depicts an "if-then" sequence to get to an intended outcome, i.e., if we provide X, the result will be Y. The ToC includes causal mechanisms to show HOW and WHY an outcome will occur. In other words, if we provide X, A will support (or hinder) a result of Y. (Connell and Kubisch 1998) (Sharp 2021) (Weiss 1995)

It makes sense then that logic models are linear and appear very structured and easy to read, as is our example in Figure 2.1 ToC components are not always linear, as effects can influence causes later. (Sharp, 2021) So the complexity of the relationships represented in a ToC creates a very messy and sometimes chaotic-looking (yet very strategic and functional!) model, like the one in Figure 2.2 below.

Fig. 2.2 Noelle's Theory of Change

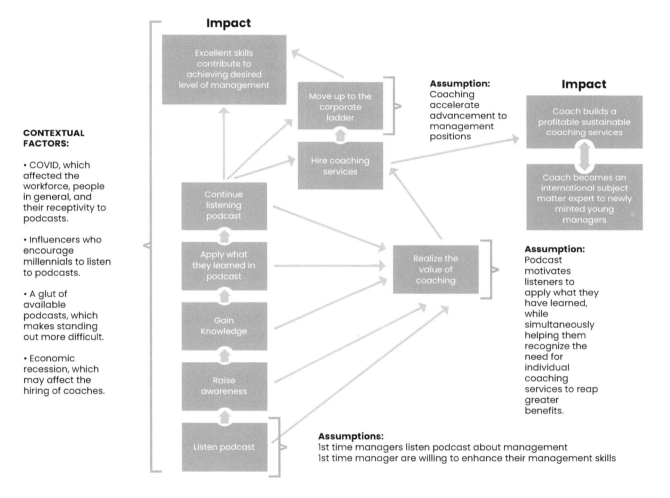

Impact

Excellent skills contribute to achieving desired level of management

Move up to the corporate ladder

Hire coaching services

Continue listening podcast

Apply what they learned in podcast

Gain Knowledge

Raise awareness

Listen podcast

Realize the value of coaching

CONTEXTUAL FACTORS:

• COVID, which affected the workforce, people in general, and their receptivity to podcasts.

• Influencers who encourage millennials to listen to podcasts.

• A glut of available podcasts, which makes standing out more difficult.

• Economic recession, which may affect the hiring of coaches.

Assumption: Coaching accelerate advancement to management positions

Impact

Coach builds a profitable sustainable coaching services

Coach becomes an international subject matter expert to newly minted young managers

Assumption: Podcast motivates listeners to apply what they have learned, while simultaneously helping them recognize the need for individual coaching services to reap greater benefits.

Assumptions:
1st time managers listen podcast about management
1st time manager are willing to enhance their management skills

Thankfully, there is no set way to draw a ToC. There are many formats to choose. So, it is up to the user to create a model that will represent the relationships among activities, the linkages between activities and outcomes, and the sequence and timing of outcomes.

We apply the concept of "backward mapping" to any ToC model. Backward mapping challenges planners to think in reverse through the specific steps needed to achieve long-term, intermediate, and early-term changes. We call this chain of events the Pathway of Change. It forms a skeleton for the other theory elements to develop.

The specific activities and events within a ToC model should be informed by rigorous research, evaluation, and expert knowledge in the relevant field. This ensures that the model accurately reflects the most effective strategies and approaches for achieving the desired short, intermediate, and long-term outcomes. For example, Noelle's goal to build a sustainable coaching business may be supported by research showing that many coaches build their practice by starting a podcast. Theories and evidence-based research will tell you how to move from one outcome to the next and, basically provide you with the order of the outcomes. Therefore, Noelle will not have to create a podcast "from scratch" because others went before her and managed to succeed. She can research what they did and replicate the steps.

But what if your project has no precedent and is completely original? In the absence of best practices or research findings on your desired subject matter, you must create the ToC for your project by articulating the hypothesis and testing it with data. You must work with others who have experience with your subject matter. Then, you and your team will work backward from your desired impact to identify the changes that need to occur first. Researching and finding support for your goals is essential to making a solid ToC model.

The ToC in Figure 2.2 outlines two impacts that Noelle hopes to achieve. One is on the top left (impact for the listener) which is for the listener to rise to their highest desired level of management as a result of using the management techniques from the podcast. The other is on the top right of the model and is an impact on Noelle, which is to build a sustainable coaching services business. The model clearly outlines, step by step, HOW to get to each outcome.

You can see arrows showing the relationships between not only the components but also the list of contextual factors and assumptions. The ToC is concerned with exactly how to reach a goal, but the contextual factors and assumptions are influential. They set the stage for the action.

ASSUMPTIONS AND CONTEXTUAL FACTORS

Assumptions and contextual factors work quietly in the wings as a backdrop for your logic model or ToC. They may or may not affect your outcomes and impact, but by acknowledging them, you will be sure to consider their effect on any successful or unsuccessful changes.

Assumptions are propositions that are taken for granted as accepted and typically represent the values, beliefs, norms, ideologies, etc., that teams and stakeholders bring to a project. They usually comprise the "rule of thumb" for various situations. (Bousselle and Champagne 2011)

A single person should not set all the assumptions for a project. The best way is to have a group of individuals identify, discuss, and articulate the assumptions within the ToC model. Also, whenever possible, back up your assumptions with data. In our example, Noelle's project to create a podcast proceeds with the following assumptions:

- Millennials listen to podcasts.
- Most first-time managers in a hybrid role come from the millennial demographic.
- Millennials listen to podcasts aimed at them and learn how to advance their career.
- To reach millennials, doing a podcast is essential.
- The podcast will lead to more coaching clients.
- The podcast will lead to speaking engagements.

Contextual factors are a set of characteristics and circumstances that interact, influence, modify, facilitate, or constrain the implementation of the project. (Meadows 2008) Context is essential because anything we plan (such as a project) will interact and connect with other people and groups within and outside an organization.

In our case, some contextual factors for Noelle's podcast may include:

- COVID-19, which affects the workforce, people in general, and their receptivity to podcasts.
- Influencers who encourage millennials to listen to podcasts.
- A glut of available podcasts, which makes standing out more difficult.
- Economic recession, which may affect the hiring of coaches.

Logic models become significantly more beneficial to users when they clearly delineate the relationships among various elements, sequentially arrange the anticipated outcomes, and thoroughly incorporate underlying assumptions and relevant contextual factors. I keep assumptions at the top of my logic model, contextual factors along the bottom, and a reminder of my Problem to Solve and Linkages at the top of my logic models. Linkages illustrate the sequence of events though which change is anticipated for the desired outcomes to occur, like shown in Figure 2.3 Noelle's Logic Model with Additional Elements.

Fig. 2.3. Noelle's Logic Model with Additional Elements

PROBLEM TO SOLVE:
First-time millennial managers in a hybrid setting require concise, digestible, and accessible managerial expertise to help them reach the next level at work.

ASSUMPTIONS:
• Millennials listen to podcasts.
• Most first-time managers in a hybrid role come from the Millennial demographic.
• Millennials will listen to a podcast aimed at them and use what they learn to help them advance in their job.
• To reach millennials internationally, doing a podcast is essential.
• The podcast will lead to more coaching clients.
• The podcast will lead to speaking engagements.

LINKAGES (sequence of events):
• Listen podcast
• Raise awareness
• Gain knowledge of management techniques
• Realize the value of professional coaching assistance. All steps lead to this event.
• Apply the management techniques learned in the podcast
• Continue listening podcast
• Listeners and those who receive coaching assistance rise to their highest desired level of management
• Podcast and/or coaching services lead to sustainable coaching practice.
• Podcast and/or coaching services contribute to Noelle becoming an international subject matter expert.

INPUTS	ACTIVITIES	OUTPUTS	OUTCOMES			IMPACT
			Short-term (1 month)	Intermediate (6 months)	Long-Term (1 year)	
.	.	.	.	.	.	.
.	.	.	.	.	.	.

CONTEXTUAL FACTORS:
• COVID, which affected the workforce, people in general, and their receptivity to podcasts.
• Influencers who encourage millennials to listen to podcasts.
• A glut of available podcasts, which makes standing out more difficult.
• Economic recession, which may affect the hiring of coaches.

However, one more element you need to know as you create a logic model for your project is your key performance indicators. For every short-term, intermediate, and long-term outcome, you should set measurable key performance indicators (KPIs).

KEY PERFORMANCE INDICATORS

As Noelle proceeds with creating her podcast, she may wonder how she knows whether or not she is achieving her outcomes. She needs to know how to measure her outcomes, track them, and analyze any negative or positive change that occurs over time. The best way to do this is by identifying Key Performance Indicators (KPI's).

KPIs are particular values, characteristics, or areas to measure outputs (products or services) and outcomes (goals). (Parameter 2019) But where do the KPIs come from? How do you determine what they are? KPIs can be determined from your outputs. In Noelle's case, the outputs shown in Figure 2.1 are number of unique listeners per episode, number of followers per episode, average percentage listened per episode, number of subscribers to the blog, days where the blog gains the biggest audience, number of positive comments reported in the blog, number of negative comments reported in the blog, and audience demographics of the blog.

You can see that all the outputs are measurable. While all outputs may serve as indicators, not all indicators are KPIs. In other words, you must choose which outputs will show progress toward your outcomes and designate them as your KPIs.

In today's podcast ecosystem, it's relatively easy to get the data for Noelle's outputs via her podcast hosting service, whether it's Apple Podcasts Connect, Google Podcast Manager, etc. Noelle also will create a blog for her podcast and can monitor traffic via Google Analytics and Google Search Console. However, whether Noelle is measuring her podcast activity or blog traffic, she must be sure her metrics measure what she wants and are critical for moving her toward her outcomes.

She also must acknowledge the challenges of podcast data. For example, knowing the number of people who download the podcast is valuable, but Noelle needs to know how many of them listened so she will have a comparative number on her audience that she can track. The number of people who listen to a show from a dedicated app like Spotify or Apple Podcasts can be measured, but not everyone will download the podcast to listen. Some will download the podcast and listen later or not at all. Obviously, Noelle must review ex-actly how a podcast hosting service may measure listenership and how they would measure the outputs she is seeking.

After researching analytics from podcast providers and reviewing her podcast outputs and outcomes, the KPIs of most interest to Noelle would be:

- Number of followers, number of listeners, number of engaged listeners (users who listened at least twenty minutes or 40 percent of an episode).
- Number of comments that address the question on the podcast blog.
- Number of calls or emails inquiring about Noelle's coaching services.

What is the reason behind Noelle's choice of these KPIs? The logical connection between the outputs of her podcast and the desired outcomes, complemented by data from her hosting service, empowers Noelle to effectively monitor her overall progress.

The next step for Noelle is to make her KPIs time bound. This approach involves setting specific timeframes for measuring KPIs. Establishing evaluation periods ensures that progress towards podcast outcomes is tracked consistently, allowing for necessary adjustments. Figure 2.1 demonstrates that Noelle has set short-term outcomes to be achieved in one-month, intermediate outcomes for six months, and a long-term outcome for one year. She can monitor progress towards these outcomes by analyzing blog comments on a weekly basis. Regarding audience growth, Noelle discovers that her podcast hosting service can provide monthly analytics for her weekly podcast. She is particularly interested in the net gain or loss of followers. To make informed decisions, she needs to see the number of followers gained, lost, and the net difference over a monthly period.

When setting your time-bound KPIs, it's important to consider the nature of each outcome, the resources available, your project's historical performance (if available), and any external factors that may impact progress towards the KPI. By doing so, organizations can ensure that their KPIs are meaningful, relevant, and actionable.

By now you should recognize how applying elements of the logic model, ToC, monitoring KPIs, and acknowledging assumptions and contextual factors will be important as you make a plan to lead an organizational transformation. The concepts you have just learned are the building blocks of the SEAM framework, which is an enhanced logic model that incorporates the ToC. SEAM is one of the best ways I've used to guide companies into digital transformation. And now, it's time to show you how it works!

All the figures and blank templates are available in appendix 1 at the end of the book.

Chapter 3

About Seam

"Every single industry is going through a major business model and technology-oriented disruption."

Aaron Levie

S EAM, as depicted in Figure 3.1, sums up my comprehensive, efficient framework for organizations and businesses to successfully transform. Anyone who directs the transformational strategy of a business or organization can use the SEAM model, which includes entrepreneurs, business owners, managers, CEOs, department heads, etc.

The framework incorporates, yet departs, from the classic logic model. Ultimately, it gives users an insightful view of their operations, where transformation is necessary, and how to create a plan to achieve it. So, before we dive in, let's talk about how SEAM differs from the logic model.

Fig. 3.1. Proprietary SEAM Comprehensive Framework

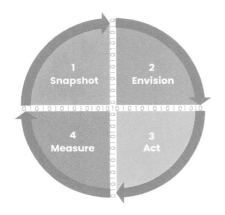

PARTS OF SEAM-ENHANCED LOGIC MODEL VS. THE LOGIC MODEL

As SEAM users make their way through the four steps, they will use an enhanced version of the logic model described in Chapter Two to point them to their desired transformation.

As shown in Figure 3.2, the SEAM model addresses aspects that are either absent from or approached differently by the logic model.

The large boxes and empty bullet points for the resources, processes, enablers, barriers, and output sections will indicate where you will fill in pertinent information for your business or organization. As indicated by arrows in Figure 3.2, each area will contribute to your outcomes and ultimate impact as you move through the SEAM model. These strategic entries may grow and change during the process of completing SEAM. As you proceed through the book, we will complete these strategic entries for Mora's Bakery and discuss them.

There also are a few places in the SEAM-enhanced logic model that provide a backdrop for the strategic entries. These aspects, although fairly stable, depict the context within which the business or organization operates. You are encouraged to fill in these parts for your specific situation, but we will not be delving into them as comprehensively as the strategic entries. These parts are indicated with a frame of dashes and include:

MISSION AND VISION: Include both elements in your model to ensure that your transformation efforts are consistent with the business's or organization's overall purpose and direction. As shown in the arrows Figure 3.2, your business or organizational outcomes should contribute to your mission and vision.

ASSUMPTIONS: These reside at the very top of the model. These assumptions might include beliefs about the organization's digital readiness, the receptiveness of the staff to change, the reliability of certain technologies, or even expectations about competitors' future strategies. The SEAM-enhanced logic model challenges you to make these assumptions explicit and recognize their influence in decision-making across the business or organization.

Fig. 3.2. SEAM-enhanced Logic Model (SEAM Model)

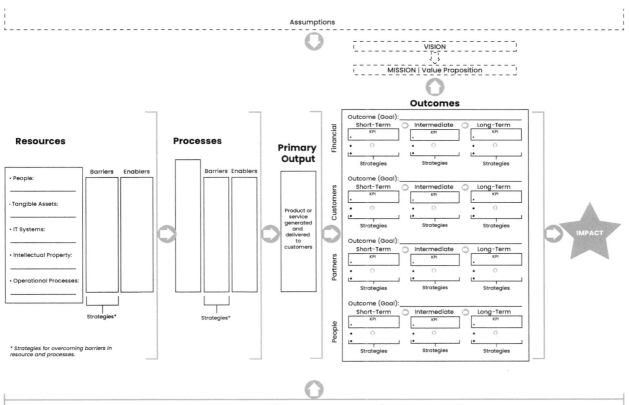

THE LANGUAGE OF THE SEAM MODEL

A notable difference between the logic model and SEAM is in the language. Here we will discuss those differences by looking at Figure 3.2.

RESOURCES: SEAM replaces the term "Inputs" with "Resources." The term "Resources" is more easily understood within the framework. For your business or organization, your resources include:

- **People:** This category includes your employees (individuals who work part-time or full-time under a contract of employment), temporary workers (individuals typically hired on a short-term basis, often through a staffing agency), and contractors (self-employed individuals or a business entity that provides services to other businesses under a specific, limited contract).
- **Tangible assets:** Your assets include the facility or office space where your organization or business conducts its operations and houses its production equipment and other physical assets, except for computers and IT hardware.

- **IT systems:** Your IT system resources include any technology necessary to run your business or organization. These include your customer relationship management (CRM) or enterprise resource planning (ERP) systems, any AI-driven applications, data analytics platforms, content management systems (CMS), project management tools, human resource management systems (HRMS), collaboration and communication tools, etc.
- **Intellectual property (IP):** These resources include any original creations or works your business or organization owns that are protected under law. These include inventions, processes, designs, symbols, logos, or any other unique and original works created specifically for your business. Examples of IP can include patents, which protect inventions and unique processes; copyrights, which protect original written works such as books, articles, or music; trademarks, which protect unique symbols or logos associated with your business; and trade secrets, which protect confidential and proprietary information. (U.S. Patent & Trademark Office, 2023)
- **Operational processes:** The policies, pro-

cedures, and workflows you have in place at your business or organization help you to succeed and, therefore, are essential resources to reach your desired outcomes. Policies, procedures, and workflows exist in every department, including operations/production, sales and marketing, human resources, finance and accounting, information technology, customer support, and administration. The SEAM model challenges the user to think through the policies, procedures, and workflows that should be in place and ask, "Do we have them? Are they working?" With such an examination, businesses and organizations can determine their needs in this area and if what they have in place is an asset or liability.

PROCESSES: SEAM replaces the term "activities" with "processes." This change honors how most organizations and businesses follow specific processes to generate products or delivered services. For example, a custom furniture manufacturing company's supply chain begins with sourcing raw materials like wood, metal, and upholstery from various suppliers. Next, skilled carpenters and artisans use raw materials to create and assemble furniture according to customer specifications. The manufacturing process may involve cutting, shaping, joining, and finishing the materials to achieve the desired design and quality. Once the furniture is complete, it is packaged and shipped to retailers, who then sell the pieces to consumers or end users.

In contrast, an online business that sells custom-designed T-shirts operates differently since it does not produce them in-house. Instead, it partners with various print-on-demand manufacturers overseas to create and ship T-shirts featuring the custom designs submitted by customers. The company maintains a website where customers can upload designs, choose a T-shirt style, and place orders. The company sends the design and order details to the print-on-demand partner, who then produces the T-shirt and ships it directly to the customer. In this scenario, the company relies heavily on e-commerce, digital marketing, and partnerships with print-on-demand manufacturers, rather than a traditional supply chain process, to facilitate sales and deliver products to customers.

Note that the term "processes" works well in the business world, while "activities" is more suitable for programs targeting changes in people's knowledge, skills, and behavior. For example, a nonprofit organization's after-school program encouraging high school students from underrepresented groups to pursue STEM college careers involve planning and implementing many activities. These may include recruitment, hands-on experiences, mentor pairing, field trips to college campus laboratories, and summer camps. Similarly, a company's diversity, equity, and inclusion (DEI) initiative may consist of several activities, such as a series of training sessions on unconscious bias, self-assessments before and after the training sessions, and a group project about mitigating biases in the workplace.

ENABLERS AND BARRIERS: Enablers are resources or processes that facilitate progress toward desired outputs or outcomes. Barriers obstruct or hinder such progress. For instance, a CRM system is an enabler because it can streamline and automate tasks and empower sales teams to focus on strategic, revenue-generating activities. An example of a barrier for a business might be a labor shortage that threatens a set production schedule. Nonprofit organizations consider grants to be enablers for their mission, while cuts in state or federal funding might present as barriers to delivering services.

PRIMARY OUTPUT: Outputs encompass final products or services and the intermediate deliverables produced at various stages of a process, system, or project. If we consider our example businesses above, the outputs for the furniture company would be the number of living room or dining room sets made. For the T-shirt company, it would be the number of custom-designed T-shirts produced. For both the organization implementing a DEI program and the nonprofit after-school STEM program, the output would be the number of attendees or participants.

For a service business like a consulting firm, there may be intermediate outputs on the way to the final deliverable. For example, an intermediate output in a financial services firm may be the research and analysis of a client's financial situation, which occurs as part of the broader output of delivering financial consulting services. In this scenario, the research and analysis become inputs for later outputs, like financial recommendations, strategies, and the final proposal to the client.

OUTCOMES: These are the results achieved through your resources and processes. Outcomes are influenced not only by the inherent capabilities of your organization or business but also by underlying assumptions (e.g., beliefs about the market, perceived customer behavior) and various contextual factors (e.g., regulatory environment, technological changes).

In SEAM, I've chosen to use the term "outcomes" instead of "goals," a decision driven by the precise evaluative capacity of outcomes. Unlike goals, which are broad and directional, outcomes offer specific, measurable, and observable indicators of whether the intended goals are being met.

Recognizing that not all outcomes can be simultaneously achieved, they are categorized as short-term, intermediate, and long-term. This allows for a phased approach towards realizing overarching goals. The timeline for achieving these outcomes is flexible and depends largely on the SEAM user. Some organizations may choose to evaluate their progress towards outcomes monthly, while others might opt for quarterly or annual assessments.

The flexibility in measurement frequency caters to diverse organizational needs, ensuring SEAM remains applicable across various contexts.

In the digital era, businesses should include customer outcomes. For a furniture company, an outcome could be customers' satisfaction derived from the quality and design of the furniture that enhances their decor and comfort. For a T-shirt company, the outcome might be the comfort, quality, and personal connection felt by customers due to the custom designs, increasing brand engagement.

These outcomes can be measured through customer satisfaction surveys (asking customers to rate their satisfaction level with the quality of the product), online reviews (analyzing the sentiment and ratings regarding product design and comfort on platforms like Google or Yelp), repeat purchases (monitoring the number of customers making more than one purchase), and brand engagement metrics (including likes, shares, comments on social media, time spent on the website, and email link clicks).

Difference Between Outputs And Outcomes: An Illustration

Everyone who uses the SEAM model must understand the fundamental difference between outputs and outcomes. These are the results achieved at the end of a process, activity, or time period. They represent the change or difference you see as a result of your efforts.

Gumbo Time

Early in my career, I worked with nonprofits in the Acadiana region of Louisiana, also known as Cajun Country. When I began explaining the parts of the SEAM model to them, I wanted to use a creative analogy to illustrate the distinction between outputs and outcomes. I chose the relatable idea of a gumbo recipe. Gumbo is the most popular dish in the region, with a rich history and diverse influences from West African, French, and Spanish cuisines. Everyone could connect with the Gumbo analogy.

Couched in the context of a bright new Cajun restaurant that serves gumbo, the principles inherent in SEAM, like outputs and outcomes, come alive. I explained that the inputs were the ingredients for the gumbo, like meat or seafood, the "holy trinity" of vegetables (onion, celery, and bell pepper), stock, and sea-

sonings. The activities included all the preparatory steps to cooking, including making the rich, creamy roux (the base of all good gumbo) and preparing the rice to accompany it. The primary output was the hearty, thick stew, cooked to perfection with all its flavors masterfully blended. The output is measured as the number of gumbo bowls per pot produced during the cooking process.

The outcome, however, extends beyond the gumbo itself to the experience it fosters. While the output is a bowl of gumbo, the true outcome lies in the comfort and warmth it brings, as it becomes a catalyst for meaningful conversations shared with friends and family over a delightful meal. Furthermore, the exceptional gumbo also generates repeat business, demonstrating its effect on customer satisfaction and loyalty.

The SEAM model encompasses financial, customer, partner, and people outcomes. The restaurant owner can measure the financial outcome, specifically sales, at various intervals such as three, six, and five years, allowing for a comprehensive assessment of performance over time. In the short term, the sales during the initial three months serve as a crucial benchmark, providing

valuable insights into the restaurant's early financial performance and indicating its potential for growth. As an intermediate financial outcome, the restaurant aims to achieve increased sales at the six-month mark, coupled with repeat business from satisfied gumbo patrons. Looking long term, a financial outcome could be to maintain profitability for five years, signifying the restaurant's sustained success.

In terms of customer outcomes, the desired long-term outcome is that past customers become loyal patrons, bringing along friends and family, and generating positive reviews for the restaurant's classic recipe. For instance, reviewers can express a deep appreciation for the gumbo recipe, noting that sharing this dish creates a sense of joy and community. This shared positive experience not only contributes to customer satisfaction but also promotes word-of-mouth advertising, ultimately attracting new patrons to the establishment.

A partner outcome could involve the restaurant owner pursuing a contract with a local supermarket chain to offer their gumbo for sale in their stores or establishing partnerships with corporate cafeterias. Lastly, a people outcome focuses on training a capable manager to assume the restaurant owner's responsibilities a few days a week, allowing for much-needed time off.

By incorporating these outcomes into the restaurant's SEAM model, the owner can effectively evaluate and track progress across financial, customer, partner, and people domains, ensuring a comprehensive approach to success and growth.

The gumbo analogy was beneficial to the people at the Cajun nonprofit. While the actual application of SEAM to their organization was much more complex, the people involved in implementing the plan would harken back to the "gumbo" metaphor if they ever became confused about outputs Zversus outcomes. The analogy helped everyone understand outputs and outcomes and their mission for the nonprofit.

KEY PERFORMANCE INDICATORS (KPIS): Organizations or businesses typically employ a mix of output KPIs and outcome KPIs to gauge their performance. Output KPIs track immediate results of processes, activities, or teams (like the number of products manufactured or services rendered), while outcome KPIs assess the effectiveness of those activities (like customer satisfaction or market share).

This dual approach enables organizations to measure operational efficiency (via output KPIs) and strategic effectiveness in achieving goals (via outcome KPIs), providing a comprehensive view of performance that informs decision-making and strategy refinement.

Importantly, KPIs often represent a key subset of outputs and outcomes chosen specifically for performance tracking and management. The selection of suitable output or outcome KPIs depends on an organization's specific context, business goals, and desired outcomes.

STRATEGIES TO REACH OUTCOMES: SEAM adopts the perspective that the development of a strategy is an ongoing process rather than a fixed long-term approach to reach outcomes. This perspective fits well with the rapid changes in technology and the uncertainty in the market. (Mankins and Gottfredson 2022) In the SEAM action plan, strategies consist of one or more activities, and these activities have specific tasks or actions that must be executed to implement the strategy. Strategy sets the direction, while activities concentrate on completing specific tasks.

CONTEXTUAL FACTORS: At the bottom of the SEAM model, there is a box to indicate contextual factors. Contextual factors indicate the conditions for the business or organization which challenge, motivate, encourage, or hinder decision-making in different areas of the operation. These may include factors that are beyond the control of the business or organization, like economic recession, COVID-19, war, governmental regulations, etc. They are important to recognize because they quietly form the backdrop for the business's activities or organization's activities. Anyone using a SEAM model should articulate their influence of such factors and be able to manage expectations for any transformation effort.

Strategies to overcome barriers: Recognizing that digital transformation is an ongoing journey rather than a static endpoint, SEAM advocates initiating this journey by planning to overcome any barriers within the resources and processes of your business or organization. This approach not only generates momentum and fosters stakeholder buy-in and support but also sets the stage for comprehensive transformation. By targeting critical challenges and emphasizing immediate gains, SEAM users can effectively drive meaningful changes.

SEAM offers a systematic and intentional approach to digital transformation, integrating seven key digital technology elements: automation, digitization, digitalization, data analytics, enhanced customer experiences, new business models, and cultural change. These elements advance SEAM's four distinct outcomes: financial, customer, partner, and people.

THE FOUR STEPS OF SEAM

I will soon introduce you to Mora, the fictitious entrepreneur behind Mora's Bakery, and we will begin journeying through the SEAM model with her business. She will move through the four steps of SEAM as described below.

SEAM STEP 1: SNAPSHOT

The Snapshot step asks, "Where is our business or organization today?" For this step, you will fill in the enhanced logic model for the SEAM framework with information from your annual plan.

The Snapshot step has three parts. Mora will begin Part 1 by documenting her current financial, customer, partner, and people KPIs and strategies. In Part 2, she will assess the bakery's resources and categorize each one as either an enabler or barrier in the context of growing and scaling her business. Finally, you'll see how Mora lists and analyzes her process components in Step 3. As she considers all the steps of the artisanal making bread process, she will visualize her process for greater clarity about her business.

SEAM STEP 2: ENVISION

The Envision step prompts you to consider, "Where do I want to take my business or organization?" In this step, Mora will explore opportunities for her bakery and how digital transformation is essential to realizing them.

The Envision step has five parts. In Part 1, Mora will begin by viewing the bakery from the customer's perspective. By understanding their desires, she can visualize the infrastructure she needs to address their requirements. Then in Part 2, Mora will articulate the impact she wants her bakery to have on the community and imagines a long-term strategy for achieving it. Fueled by new insight, Mora will move on to Part 3 of Envision to consider how she can overcome her barriers to success through digital transformation. In Part 4, she will examine the outcomes, KPIs, and strategies. Finally, in Part 5, she maps out the future and her five-year plan for lifting her barriers and achieving her outcomes.

With her Envision step complete, Mora is ready for action with the Act step!

SEAM STEP 3: ACTION

The Act step tackles the question, "How do we get to where we want to go?" In the Act step, Mora develops and executes an action plan to transform the business she envisions in SEAM Step 2. She then creates action plans to reach her desired outcomes while concurrently transforming her business with technology.

Mora begins the three-part Act step by implementing a particular technique used by the military to ensure that her strategies will be effective. We will then see how Mora considers and chooses the right project management tool to align her team with her goals in Part 2 of the Act step. Throughout the Act step, Mora will list the strategies, identify the activities to achieve each outcome, and the tasks required for each activity. In Part 3, she will execute them. How will she do? You'll have to read to find out!

SEAM STEP 4: MEASURE

The Measure step answers, "How effective was my action plan?" In this step, Mora analyzes her progress in SEAM Year 1, Year 2, and Year 3. She will measure the bakery's progress toward her financial, customer, partner, and people outcomes and see if her transformation is moving her closer to what she wants. She will chart how her progress toward digital transformation will unfold in each SEAM year to meet her desired outcomes. Most importantly, Mora will learn how vital measurement is and how the results can generate even more growth!

USING THE SEAM FRAMEWORK

My clients highly value the SEAM framework for its visual focus. The 4-step SEAM framework simplifies the transformation process, making it a less daunting challenge. An in-house management team can use the framework to guide one or two departments through small-scale yet critical steps to begin the transformation journey, or outside consultants can use it to create a shift across the entire organization.

Whether to work through the SEAM framework alone or with a team depends on the decision-making authority of the team members, as well as the entrepreneur or business owner's personal preference and specific circumstances. It is important to carefully consider the potential benefits and drawbacks of involving the team in applying the framework. In some cases, involving the team can lead to compromise and a failure to plan for what the entrepreneur truly wants. Additionally, an entrepreneur's ego may prevent them from addressing embarrassing problems that need solving in the team's presence. However, in other cases, involving the team can provide valuable insights and perspectives that can enhance the framework's effectiveness. Ultimately, it is up to the entrepreneur or small business owner to decide how best to approach the SEAM framework based on their unique situation and goals.

Embarking on a digital transformation journey can be challenging, but its benefits offer improved efficiency, customer service, and competitive advantage are immense. Investing in a consultant or having someone on the staff with the right skills and knowledge can simplify your digital transformation.

CONSULTANTS OR SPECIALIZED STAFF MEMBERS

Transforming your business or organization with digital technology is a complex process that requires an in-depth understanding of both technology and business operations. It's not simply about implementing new technology but about fundamentally changing how a business operates and delivers value to its customers. Therefore, having a guide in this process, be it a consultant or a dedicated staff member, can provide immense benefits.

Consultants are always available to help with SEAM. However, going through SEAM alone can be a valuable precursor to finding a consultant. Working through SEAM in preparation for working with a consultant will help you identify where you require help the most and pinpoint the best kind of consultant to hire. It will save valuable time and money starting with the first meeting.

Consultants can be immensely valuable for many reasons. They can provide knowledge and experience you do not have and can guide you in applying the latest trends and technologies to drive impact and eliminate missteps. Since consultants view your business through fresh eyes, they can offer a critical eye-opening perspective on your activities. During a digital transformation, they can reduce the time it takes to implement your technology and bring your business or organization up to speed on the new systems.

Remember that there are no shortcuts when it comes to transforming your organization or business. Transformation has a starting point but not necessarily a final destination. Digital transformation is a journey that takes time, intention, and perseverance and can take you in many different directions. Don't be sold on buzzwords or false promises from anyone who claims to know what you need before examining what you have. Transformation is only possible with a predetermined strategy customized to your desired outcomes. SEAM provides a way for businesses and organizations to create that personalized solution.

Any consultant will see the value of the SEAM framework if you share it as your preferred method to aid in your transformation.

SEAM AND YOUR OPERATION

Remember that before jumping into any organizational transformation, your plan should align with your organization's mission and vision. Digital transformation can lead to new opportunities for improvement and growth, but it is crucial to recognize that many organizations struggle or even fail in their efforts. Factors such as resistance to change, unclear goals or strategy, and inadequate resources or expertise can pose significant challenges to successful digital transformation. The SEAM 4-step framework helps you to approach digital transformation with a clear plan and strategy that evaluates your current state, identifies readiness for digital transformation, develops an effective plan, and monitors its implementation with the flexibility to make the necessary adjustments. Also, most businesses or organizations have ROI in mind for their long-term outcome. With an expected ROI in mind, your team can set a workable budget for your transformation with some "wiggle room" to increase funding, if necessary.

A SEAM EXAMPLE: MORA'S BAKERY

How does this all come together for a business or organization as they work toward digital transformation?

Mora's experience is a composite of many of the clients I've helped. Her struggles will strike a chord with you, whether you operate in a Business-to-Consumer (B2C) market or have a Business-to-Business (B2B) enterprise, both of which could be product- or service-ori-

ented. This book will also address how those involved in various types of organizations, including nonprofits, can apply the framework.

THE STORY OF MORA'S BAKERY

Like many of us, Mora said "yes" to the opportunity to become an entrepreneur. Her business was born out of her passion for baking, necessity, and a deep desire to control what she does for a living. Does any of that sound familiar? Here is how Mora got started.

Mora Moritz was a young girl growing up in a small town in Ohio when her aunt first taught her to make bread by hand. It didn't take Mora long to fall in love with breadmaking. She married, had three children, and kept up her aunt's traditional recipes and techniques to make delicious bread for her family and very appreciated gifts for those around her. She dreamed of running a bakery, but she was too busy with life to follow that dream.

Then ten years ago, tragedy struck when her husband suddenly died of a heart attack. Left widowed with young children to support, Mora decided life was too short not to pursue her dream. With her aunt's signature recipes in hand, Mora obtained a loan and opened a bakery in her town.

Mora's Bakery soon developed

a cult following who appreciated her quality ingredients, distinctive taste, and flavor. Soon, Mora could no longer do it alone. She hired a small staff and divided her operation into mixing and baking shifts to keep up with daily orders taken during the week.

Mora's clientele is diverse, encompassing national supermarket chains, local independent grocery stores, and several restaurants. She still makes her bread by hand and uses more expensive, natural ingredients for its unique taste. She sells hot dog, hamburger, hoagie, slider buns, sliced bread, baguettes, dinner rolls, focaccias, brioche, and ciabattas. People love that the bread bakes in a dairy and nut-free facility. Mora evolved her line to include bread for vegans and developed a niche for people with special dietary needs.

MORA'S CHALLENGES

LABOR TROUBLES: Mora struggles with the high cost of labor, management, and turnover. Since nobody will work for minimum wage, Mora pays more. However, turnover is still high at the bakery. Mora attributes this to her inability to find a consistent management team or someone who can supervise the entire production process at a salary Mora can afford.

The culture is friendly and familiar at the bakery, which makes it harder for managers to implement new controls. New managerial hires are unclear about their role because many processes are not automated or formalized. For example, proofing is not temperature-controlled, so it is up to the baker to decide when the bread has risen enough. Because the bread is handmade, the product needs to be more consistent, and there is more waste in production. Mora donates what she can't sell.

Mora has two people in the bakery who have been with her a long time and have earned her trust. She expects that these two individuals will help her implement the SEAM framework. She plans to invest in their training and management skills so they will be able to take her place in training the new hires and managing staff. The time Mora spends managing new employees eats into the time she needs for marketing or strategic planning. Then, when the new employees work more slowly or make mistakes, it dips into the bakery's profitability.

Mora's town has many immigrants. When

people first arrive, they are happy to work at the bakery but soon leave for less strenuous work or a better opportunity elsewhere. People must be in good condition to stand for nearly their entire shift, so younger workers stay longer. Unfortunately, though, the heartier locals who Mora can afford to hire and can physically do the work show no interest in working at the bakery.

RETAIL WOES: The bakery's retail business, which serves national supermarket chains, has a fluctuating income pattern – sometimes it brings in a reasonable income, at other times it underperforms, and occasionally, it does exceptionally well. Despite this inconsistency, Mora firmly believes that her sales have the potential to soar much higher. The stores want Mora to lower the price of her bread, but she cannot do it. She lacks the economy of scale and automated production processes to reduce costs. Her bread costs more to make because the natural ingredients cost more. Her sales volume is lower, so sometimes she doesn't cover delivery costs. Since Mora's Bakery does not use preservatives, the shelf life for her artisanal bread ranges from a few days to a week, depending on the bread product and the store's humidity and temperature.

The bakery must check the store shelves weekly to remove expired products.

Mora's competition uses artificial ingredients and preservatives to enhance color, flavor, and texture. Their bread costs less and has a much longer shelf life. These more prominent manufacturers also have been in the market longer and have the financial resources to grow their sales teams, facilities, and more. Mora knows she has a place in the market but still needs to address her challenges.

SEAM AND MORA'S BAKERY

Can a digital transformation address Mora's challenges? The SEAM framework was the right tool to guide her through the changes she needed. Let's continue to the next chapter and see how Mora starts applying the first step of the SEAM model, the Snapshot, to her bakery. While her situation is most likely different from yours, you will follow the same thought process when you use SEAM to transform your business or organization.

All the figures and blank templates are available in appendix 1 at the end of the book.

Chapter 4

SEAM Step 1: SNAPSHOT

"If you want to maximize your total potential... you have to know yourself first."

Mark McGwire

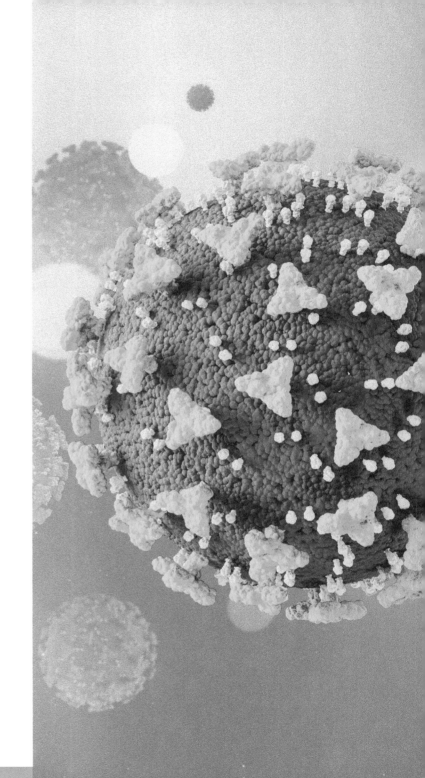

The first letter in SEAM stands for Snapshot. Taking a mental "snapshot" of the current state of your company may sound elementary. However, it is the foundation of your digital transformation.

In an ideal world, your business moves forward based on a well-thought-out business plan. A company can then "work as planned" with clarity for everyone in the organization regarding their roles, responsibilities, and processes for the business to succeed. In the real world, unforeseen circumstances often make deviating from the original plan necessary.

During the COVID-19 pandemic, companies had to pivot their products and services virtually overnight to address the disruptions to supply chains, staffing, and business operations. Many strategic plans were cast aside in the chaos, and "survival mode" took over. There was no time to document new processes. Instead of "work as planned," teams performed work as they could get done in the most effective, productive way possible. Instead of "work as planned," they performed "work as done," which often involves shortcuts, workarounds, and making changes in processes without documentation. (Kolb and Rubin 1984) (Larson and Gray 2021) The merit of "work as done" is effective in the short term. However, it's often unsustainable and can ultimately prevent a business from achieving its long-term outcomes.

WHY A SNAPSHOT?

The Snapshot helps clarify the discrepancy in the business between "work as planned" and "work as done." It is a dedicated step toward describing the current situation of the organization. The Snapshot is valuable for many other reasons, too.

THE SNAPSHOT CREATES A BASELINE TO MEASURE PROGRESS: It allows us to see how our business operates at a specific time. From this baseline, we can measure progress, making it the starting point to complete an entire SEAM model.

THE SNAPSHOT UNCOVERS IMPORTANT ISSUES: By taking a deep dive into how the organization works, the Snapshot identifies discrepancies in standard operating procedures and deviations from original project plans. Most importantly, the Snapshot reveals opportunities for improvement, including the potential for automation or integration of digital technologies.

THE SNAPSHOT REVEALS THE VALUE OF THE TEAM'S WORK: As team leaders delegate more work to their teams, it is common to lose sight of their responsibilities. (Lai 2018) However, everyone wants their work to be meaningful. Examining the actual contribution of your team at each step of the company's processes can help you understand the value and meaning of their work. Taking the time to learn more about your team's roles and responsibilities shows respect and solidarity with them.

THE SNAPSHOT REVEALS YOUR OPTIONS: When a business owner or organization leader delves into their business and discovers its strengths and challenges, they may consider different options for the future. Mora will do this in her example after she completes the Snapshot step of SEAM.

MORA'S SNAPSHOT

The Snapshot for your business will look different than the one for Mora's. However, you will follow the same procedure she does to fill in your own SEAM model.

Mora's first step in creating her Snapshot is to fill out the components as numbered in Figure 4.1 You can see in the financial outcome section that Mora tracks progress towards her annual outcomes every quarter. When completing the Snapshot for your business, modify or adapt the outcome part of the model to align with the time frame you use to monitor progress (i.e., daily, weekly, monthly, or annually).

SEAM STEP 1: SNAPSHOT

PART 1: Documenting Outcomes, KPIs, and Strategies

PART 2: Listing and Categorizing Resources

PART 3: Listing and Categorizing Process Components

Fig. 4.1. SEAM Step 1: Snapshot

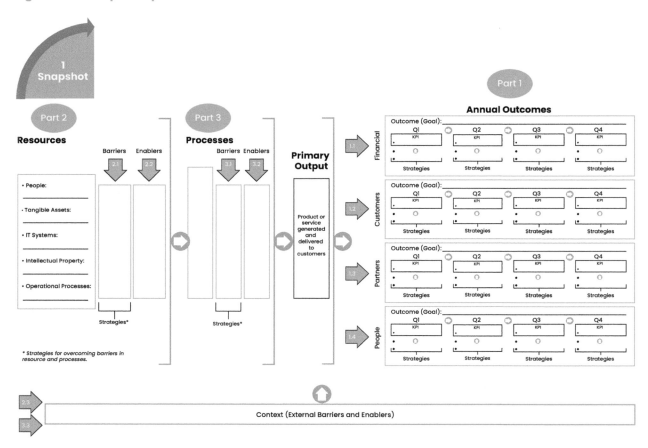

The order in which you fill out the elements of the Snapshot is important and begins with outcomes.

SNAPSHOT PART 1: DOCUMENTING OUTCOMES, KPIS, AND STRATEGIES

Mora begins by inputting her annual goals from her business plan into the outcome component of the model, and it is where you will start your Snapshot as well. There are four types of outcomes in the SEAM model: financial, customers, partners, and people. We'll start with the financial outcomes.

FINANCIAL OUTCOMES
(Snapshot 1.1)

This first part of the SEAM model asks you to consider the financial outcomes of your business. What KPIs does your business or organization currently use to measure progress toward achieving them? How frequently are the KPIs assessed—weekly, monthly, quarterly, or annually?

Mora's annual financial outcome for her bakery is to increase revenue from $1,686,250 to $2,035,277.50. She broke the year into four quarters and developed a KPI for each to monitor progress toward her annual outcome. Mora documents her KPIs using the financial reports from her accounting software and then inputs the data into an Excel dashboard.

Some common KPIs that businesses monitor include:

- Growth in revenue (Mora's KPI in Figure 4.2 is an example)
- Net profit margin
- Gross profit margin
- Operational cash flow
- Current accounts receivables
- Inventory turnover
- Earnings before interest, taxes, depreciation, and amortization (EBITDA)
- Cost of goods sold (COGS)

Mora also monitors COGS weekly and gross profit margin monthly in an Excel file. COGS refers to the cost of raw materials, labor costs directly tied to production, and any other direct expenses incurred during bread production. A high value for COGS can be indicative of inefficiencies in the bakery. Inefficiencies can jeopardize the bakery's ability to pay its bills on time, increase product costs, and ultimately force a price hike on the bread that will reduce sales. Mora also breaks down

COGS into specific components to identify where the cost is higher than expected, as shown below.

- Cost of ingredients (This is hard for Mora to control because her supplier controls the prices)
- Cost of production
- Cost of packing labor
- Cost of distribution

Mora pays close attention to the gross profit margin to know how much of the revenue remains as profit after accounting for COGS. A higher gross margin percentage indicates that the bakery generates more revenue for each dollar spent on producing the bread, which suggests better production efficiency and cost management. On the other hand, a lower gross margin percentage may signal higher production costs, inefficiencies, or pricing issues.

Mora did a good job writing her financial KPIs in her business plan. They are specific, clear, and measurable. Figure 4.2 shows how Mora wrote her financial outcome and KPIs in the SEAM model:

Fig. 4.2. Annual Financial Outcome for Mora's Bakery

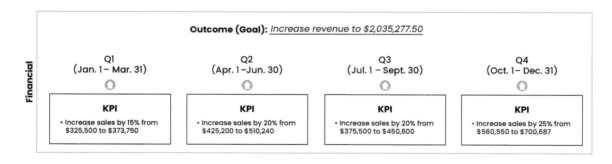

Perhaps you are filling out your SEAM model for a nonprofit organization. Your financial outcomes might be incoming donations. A service business like an accounting firm may have business expenses like software and IT, but not COGs as Mora does. Regardless of your type of business or organization, your financial KPIs should take into account four elements that make them easier to track and evaluate. They are:

Timeframe: Mora's KPIs indicate a specific performance period to achieve $2,035,277.50 in sales by Q4. Each quarter has a start and end date to monitor progress (e.g., the first quarter has $373,750) and make necessary adjustments throughout the year. As you fill out your model, be sure that you include a clear timeframe for your outcomes and KPIs.

Target level of performance: Mora clearly states the KPI's target for each quarter—to increase sales by 15, 20, or 25 percent. In selecting the percentage increase for each quarter, she considered the bakery's past sale performance, current trends in healthy food choices of millennials and Generation Z, and marketing campaigns she wrote as a strategy to reach her targets. How will you determine your target level of performance? What information will you consider?

Baseline: Mora uses last year's sales for each quarter as a reference point. For example, for the first quarter, the baseline is $325,500. You must use your previous sales data for your baseline as well.

Data source: Mora uses her dashboard reports from the past year and hard copies of financial statements before COVID-19 from her accountant. What source will you use?

When selecting a target percentage increase, consider your past performance, market conditions, industry trends, and organizational strategy. Because of Mora's continuous sales cycle, she can track and achieve her KPIs quarterly. However, some businesses have longer sales cycles. For example, those involved in manufacturing complex electronic components may opt to set a KPI timeframe of six months because it may take that long to complete the product development process.

When you insert your outcomes and KPIs in the SEAM model, write them as they appear in your business plan. If your KPIs are not specific like Mora's, that is okay. You will revise them or develop new ones with all the elements listed above in Step 2 of SEAM.

CUSTOMER OUTCOMES
(Snapshot 1.2)

Customer outcomes are different than customer satisfaction. While customer satisfaction is a commonly acknowledged metric, businesses now increasingly focus on customer outcomes. (Zeithaml, Bitner, and Gremler 2017) This shift reflects a broader understanding of the importance of doing more than simply meeting customer expectations. Today's consumers expect businesses and organizations to deliver tangible results that create long-term value for them, strengthen their relationships, and earn their loyalty. (Denning 2018) (Kotler and Keller 2016)

Both customer outcomes and customer satisfaction focus on the customer's experience with a product or service, but they differ in scope and focus. Customer outcomes refer to the results or benefits customers experience as a consequence of purchasing or using a product or service. On the other hand, customer satisfaction is a measure of how well a product or service meets or exceeds a custom-er's expectations. It is a subjective evaluation that can be influenced by various factors, such as the quality of the product or service and the customer's prior experiences and expectations.

As the focus on customer centricity continues to grow and businesses increasingly recognize the importance of measuring customer outcomes, it is essential to identify the right KPIs to track and measure success. Here are some examples of KPIs for different customer outcomes (Zeithaml, Bitner, and Gremler 2017) (Payne, Frow, and Eggert 2017)

- *Outcome:* Improved performance or productivity. *KPI:* Time saved per customer interaction or task completion. This KPI may be useful if your product or service enables the customer to achieve better results, complete tasks more efficiently, or save time.
- *Outcome:* Cost savings. *KPI:* Reduction in expenses or increase in value for money. This is an often easily measured, valuable KPI if your product or service can help customers save money or provide better value for the price.
- *Outcome:* Emotional satisfaction. *KPI:* Improvement in customer's emotional

state, such as joy, happiness, or stress relief. Use this KPI if your product or service can meet the customer's emotional needs and create a positive experience.

- **Outcome:** Enhanced convenience. **KPI:** Routine tasks or steps simplified/automated for the customer. If your product or service can simplify the customer's life by helping them communicate, eat on the go, schedule their time better, or complete tasks more easily, this is an appropriate KPI.
- **Outcome:** Social benefit. **KPI:** Number of community events hosted or sponsored by the company. Just as simplifying routine tasks can enhance convenience for the customer, hosting or sponsoring community events can contribute to the well-being of the community. Setting this KPI can provide insights on how your customers perceive your product or service's contribution to the local community.

As we can see, there are challenges to measuring some of these customer outcomes. For example, it is hard to quantify intangible aspects, such as customer emotions and feelings. It is also challenging to maintain business profitability while trying to meet customer ex-

pectations and deliver personalized products and services. Businesses are adopting intelligent agent technologies (IATs) to gain a competitive edge and respond more adeptly to market challenges. IATs enable companies to scan the market landscape efficiently. This includes keeping a vigilant eye on competitors' strategies, understanding customer preferences, and continuously evaluating the effectiveness of the firm's own initiatives to address emerging challenges. (Kumar et. al. 2021)

In addition to IATs, companies are also harnessing the power of CRM tools. CRM tools provide businesses with invaluable insights through data analytics and automation. CRM tools facilitate a deeper understanding of customer interactions by meticulously tracking and analyzing the experiences that customers have with products or services. This, in turn, empowers businesses to fine-tune their offerings and deliver a more personalized and satisfying customer experience. (Buttle 2009)

However, it is essential to recognize that AI and CRM are not standalone solutions. Instead, they are complementary tools that support a comprehensive customer-centric strategy, encompassing effective communication, employee training, and organizational commitment to prioritizing customer needs and expectations.

Mora does not measure satisfaction nor the value of the nutritional aspects of her bread among her customers (national supermarket chains, local independent grocery stores, and restaurants). But she does have anecdotal evidence that her restaurant customers like her bread. The delivery employee told her that some restaurant owners told him they liked the flavor and freshness of the bread.

Mora tracks the following outputs as part of the quality control of the distribution process.

- Orders completed
- Orders shipped
- Orders delivered in full on time
- Cost of quality correction—rejection of products
- Complaints resolved (or not resolved) on the first call
- Calls answered the first time (not having to be transferred to another party)

Since Mora only has anecdotal evidence in terms of customer satisfaction, these measurable outputs help her to extrapolate how well her products are satisfying customers. All of them indicate a customer demand or the customer experience of interacting with Mora's Bakery.

PARTNER OUTCOMES
(Snapshot 1.3)

Next is a place to record the outcomes and KPIs for partners. Partners are the businesses in your industry that collaborate with you on various levels through strategic alliances, joint marketing efforts, or sharing resources. Partnerships often involve a mutual exchange of value, where both businesses benefit from supporting each other, or offer complementary services to enhance each other's offerings. For example, you may borrow inventory from another business when you run low. You could consider the business a partner, and you may set a KPI to reduce those emergency loans. Another example of a partnership is when two complementary companies serve as referral sources for each other. For instance, you could own a catering business and refer your clients to an event planning company. You could set KPIs to increase the number of events the two companies work together for the year.

Some partnerships are formalized through contracts or a memorandum of understanding (MOU). Others are simply verbal. You could articulate an outcome to formalize the collaboration with other businesses through MOU. The MOU is a non-binding agreement between two or more parties that outlines the terms and details of their collaboration, mutual responsibilities, and shared goals. It is often used as a preliminary step before entering into a more formal, legally binding contract.

Here are examples of partner outcomes and associated KPIs.

- *Outcome:* Enhanced lead generation and conversion. *KPI:* Conversion rate of partner referrals, which measures the effectiveness of the partnership in generating qualified leads and converting them into contracts or closed deals. By tracking the number of referrals from the partner that successfully result in a signed contract, you can evaluate the quality of leads provided by the partner and the overall success of the partnership in driving new business opportunities. A higher conversion rate indicates a more fruitful collaboration regarding lead generation and conversions.

- *Outcome:* Increased sales for both partners. *KPI:* Percentage increase in sales revenue for each partner, which measures the increase in sales revenue for both partners. Comparing the percentage of sales increase before and after the partnership can provide insights into the success of the collaboration.

- *Outcome:* Expanded market reach. *KPI:* Number of new cities in the county where the two businesses are doing work, which measures the partnership's success in terms of geographical expansion and reaching new local markets.

- *Outcome:* Improved products offerings. *KPI:* Number of new products developed through the partnership, which measures the innovation and value-add that the partnership brings to each company's service portfolio. A higher number of new products developed jointly indicates a successful collaboration in terms of product innovation.

- *Outcome:* Enhanced brand reputation. *KPI:* Increase in positive brand sentiment, which measures the improvement in brand perception and reputation for both partner companies because of the partnership. Tracking the increase in positive brand sentiment through customer feedback, reviews, and social media engagement, can help partners evaluate the impact of their alliance on their brand reputation.

Mora does have a verbal agreement with a smaller, artisanal bakery. They collaborate to meet orders when one of them needs help, but this information is not in her business plan. For now, Mora leaves the partner KPI part of the SEAM model blank. Likewise, if your business or organization does not have a partnership agreement with other businesses, leave it blank.

PARTNERS VS. SUPPLIERS: It is important to distinguish between partners and suppliers, even though both may play a significant role in your business operations. Due to disruptions in the supply chain, Mora considers the suppliers of her bread ingredients to be her partners and maintains weekly communication with them to ensure she receives her order on time for the correct price. She documents her conversations in a notepad. Some of her providers have IT systems; Mora enters orders and follows up online.

In our discussions with Mora, we agreed not to consider them partners because suppliers are typically not involved in the business's strategic decision-making or collaborative efforts. They primarily focus on delivering the necessary materials and ensuring the quality and consistency of their products or services.

As you categorize those businesses or organizations essential to your enterprise, make sure you categorize them as partners only if they are true stakeholders in your success.

PEOPLE OUTCOMES
(Snapshot 1.4)

People are the most vital asset of any business or organization, forming the foundation upon which success is built. They drive product development, service delivery, customer relations, and overall operational efficiency. Their knowledge, skills, and dedication directly impact the company's growth and profitability.

People KPIs measure how your employees, temporary workers, consultants, and contractors affect your business or organization. As you read the example outcomes and KPIs below, consider how they may translate to your business or organization and which ones you should include in your SEAM model.

- **Outcome:** Improved employee productivity. **KPI:** Output per employee. This measures the overall productivity of each employee by comparing the output (e.g., units produced, tasks completed, or sales closed) to the total number of employees. A higher output per employee indicates increased efficiency and productivity in the workplace.
- **Outcome:** Enhanced employee engagement. **KPI:** Employee engagement score. This measures the level of engagement and commitment among employees using surveys or questionnaires that assess factors such as job satisfaction, work environment, and alignment with company values. A higher employee engagement score indicates a more motivated and committed workforce.
- **Outcome:** Reduced employee turnover. **KPI:** Employee retention rate. This tracks the percentage of employees who remain with the company over a period (e.g., one year). A higher employee retention rate suggests that the company successfully retains talent, which can positively impact overall performance and reduce recruitment costs.
- **Outcome:** Improved employee skill development. **KPI:** Number of completed training programs or certifications. This measures the effectiveness of the company's training and development initiatives by tracking the number of employees who complete training programs or obtain professional certifications. More earned certificates and diplomas indicate a more skilled and capable workforce.

One of Mora's main challenges is employee turnover. She tracks staff turnover by type (resignations, end of contract, terminations) and by each step of her production and distribution process (purchasing, mixing, shaping dough, baking, packaging, and distribution).

In Figure 4.3, Mora has filled in the "people" section of the model with the intention of decreasing staff turnover. Her outcome is ambitious, as she intends to reduce staff turnover by 50 percent in Q2 and Q3.

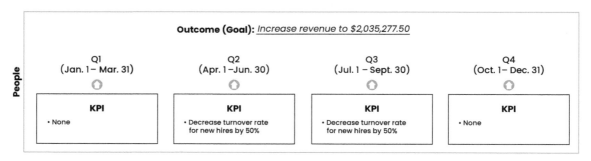

Fig. 4.3. Annual People Outcome for Mora's Bakery

STRATEGIES TO ACHIEVE OUTCOMES
(Snapshot 1.1–1.4)

Next, Mora must fill in the strategies for each outcome type in Snapshot 1.1-1.4. However, the items Mora listed in her annual business plan are activities, not strategies. This is common for many businesses and organizations, and you also should check whether your business plan outlines activities or actual strategies.

What is the difference? Strategies are high-level, long-term plans for achieving a specific outcome (goal), while activities are the specific tasks or actions that must be executed to implement the strategy. Strategy focuses on decision-making and setting overall direction, while activities concentrate on completing specific tasks.

The purpose of the Snapshot step is to put in the model whatever you have in your plan, so this is what she did. In Figure 4.4, you can see how Mora outlines activities to help achieve the two outcomes in her annual plan. Every outcome requires at least one strategy outlined in the model. Notice that Mora left it blank. She will fill in the strategy in the Step 2 of SEAM.

Fig. 4.4. Activities to Achieve Bakery's Outcomes

Outcome (Goal): _Increase revenue to $2,035,277.50_

Financial

Strategies: _____

Activities:

- Hire a digital marketing company with a proven record of using the best analytic techniques to target customers.
- Leverage existing connections with national chain supermarkets to get into other supermarkets.
- Reach out to the new restaurants that have recently opened near the new headquarters of the large multinational company.
- Sell directly to consumers via the website.

Outcome (Goal): _Decrease staff turnover_

People

Strategies: _____

Activities:

- Partner with two vocational schools to provide work experience.
- Partner with high schools to create a training program for the summer.
- Provide incentives for staff who bring in additional personnel to work at the bakery.

A word about strategies, they should be supported by reliable data sources, demonstrating they have been proven effective in the past and apply to the current situation. In the absence of such evidence, it is crucial to communicate the potential risks involved, ensuring that all stakeholders are aware of the uncertainties.

Sometimes strategies are formalized, put on paper, and issued as a formal declaration. Other times, strategies are informal. They may be born from an office meeting or emerge at a dinner out of the office. In either instance, everyone must be on board with the strategy (through formal means) before devoting resources to implement it.

ANECDOTAL EVIDENCE FOR STRATEGIES: Anecdotes are sometimes all we have to inspire a strategy. However, when the anecdote is from a dissatisfied customer, their personal story can affect us in a way that clouds our judgment. Suppose you are a clothing manufacturer who receives a complaint from a customer that your clothing gave them a terrible rash. Even if it was the first-ever complaint in the history of your company, the weight of the claim may panic you into spending time and energy trying to find out how the clothing could have caused a rash. It is easy to overlook that the complaint was one in a million, and the customer may have extremely sensitive skin or even wore the clothes against a doctor's advice. Anecdotes become troublesome when they resonate with us so emotionally that we overemphasize negative data points. If we incorrectly weigh the complaint's negative, emotional information, we can choose the wrong strategy, leading to a loss of customers and valuable resources. (Teixeira 2017)

A better way to use anecdotal information is to let it elicit questions that can lead to better processes and considerations. Is there a growing allergy to the material fibers used in the clothing that the customer ordered? Was there anything particularly wrong with the clothing from the lot the customer received? Could an allergen have contaminated the clothing before it was shipped? These questions can help test whether the anecdotal evidence is valuable before letting the experience color your strategies and KPIs.

In Mora's case, anecdotal evidence can inspire some of her strategies. For example, perhaps Mora heard from a parent that her son in college would welcome a job at the bakery. Mora could create a strategy to recruit student helpers based on that anecdotal evidence, but the strategy may or may not work. The parent may be mistaken about their son wanting to work at the bakery, or the son already may have found a different job. However, if Mora seeks out information first—like contacting the college and finding out that students have been asking for culinary job opportunities—she could initiate the strategy based on that evidence.

SNAPSHOT PART 2: LISTING AND CATEGORIZING RESOURCES

In Snapshot Figure 4.1, you must list your resources (Part 2). Anything your business utilizes in managing, producing, and delivering goods or services is considered a resource. SEAM divides resources into people, tangible assets (space and equipment only), IT systems, IP, and operational processes. Here are some examples of what may be considered resources in each category for your particular business or organization.

People: These include employees, temporary workers, consultants (expert advisors), and contractors (with a clear scope of work and deliverables).

Tangible assets: All facilities, machinery, equipment for production, vehicles, and other physical assets, excluding computers and IT hardware, comprise your tangible assets.

IT systems: These examples include Customer Relationship Management (CRM), Enterprise Resource Planning (ERP) systems, AI-driven applications, data analytics platforms, Content Management Systems (CMS), project management tools, Human Resource Management Systems (HRMS), and collaboration and communication tools.

Intellectual property: Your IP includes any patents, copyrights, trademarks, etc.

Operational processes: These are defined as policies, procedures, or workflows for key functional areas like operations/production, sales and marketing, human resources, finance and accounting, IT, customer support, and administration. When you list these items, you do not have to list them in detail. Ask yourself, do I have them? And if so, are they paper or electronic?

As you fill your resources in the SEAM model, as done in Figure 4.5, you can use generalities like Mora did (i.e., essential equipment for making the bread) rather than listing everything in detail. It would get overwhelming to do that! The same rule applies to people, IT systems, IP, and operational processes. The point of the exercise is to broadly inventory your resources so you can see where you could improve your position or use your resources more wisely. Point to see how much automation and AI is in your company.

Fig. 4.5. Listing Resources of Mora's Bakery

Resources

- **People:** Employees, temporary workers, consultants, and contractors.
- **Tangible Assets:** Facility and essential equipment for each step of the bread-making process (e.g., oven, dough mixer).
- **IT Systems:** None. Excel dashboard to track financial KPIs.
- **Intellectual Property** None. However, the bread recipes are time-tested recipes that have gained widespread popularity over the years.
- **Operational Processes:** Paper and electronic versions for production, human resources, finance and accounting, and administration.

If you are a consultant or a service business, you will most likely be unable to list many tangible assets, like equipment, among your resources. However, you may have an accounting software program you can list under IT systems.

Under IP, Mora cannot list anything. Her recipes are valuable resources, but bread recipes cannot be copyrighted or patented under U.S. copyright law. (U.S. Copyright Office, 2021) However, your business or organization may have original works such as patents, publications, symbols, names, and logos used in commerce and can all be trademarked and listed as IP.

CATEGORIZE BARRIERS AND ENABLERS
(Snapshot 2.1–2.2)

After listing her resources, Mora must review each resource and categorize it as either an enabler or barrier. She then can list them in Parts 2.1 and 2.2 of Figure 4.6 you must do the same with your own list of resources for your business or organization, by determining if each resource is a barrier or enabler. A resource cannot be both an enabler and a barrier.

As you do this for your business or organization, as Mora does in Figure 6, use adjectives to categorize why the resource is an enabler or a barrier. For example, instead of listing "equipment" in the barrier section, Mora specified "old ovens with inconsistent temperature control." Mora's more detailed descriptions give us a good picture of the strengths and weaknesses of Mora's Bakery. At the bottom of Figure 4.6,

Part 2.3, Mora describes the external factors beyond her control that could influence the bakery and categorizes them as barriers and enablers. She will complete this list of contextual factors in the next section when she outlines her bread-making process. This is just the starting point.

Fig. 4.6. Categorizing Bakery's Resources into Barriers or Enablers

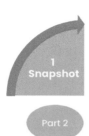

Resources

- **People:** Employees, temporary workers, consultants, and contractors.
- **Tangible Assets:** Facility and essential equipment for each step of the bread-making process (e.g., oven, dough mixer).
- **IT Systems:** None. Excel dashboard to track financial KPIs.
- **Intellectual Property** None. However, the bread recipes are time-tested recipes that have gained widespread popularity over the years.
- **Operational Processes:** Paper and electronic versions for production, human resources, finance and accounting, and administration.

Barriers

- **People:**
  - High cost of labor
  - Employee turnover, including management team
- **Tangible Assets:**
  - Old ovens with inconsistent temperature control
- **IT Systems:**
  - Lacks automated system
  - Has not integrated technology into bread-making process, including a lack of digital solutions
- **Operational Processes:**
  - No written or incomplete electronic versions for production, sales and marketing, human resources, finance and accounting, IT, customer support, and administration
  - No written or incomplete electronic training protocols available

Enablers

- **Tangible Assets:** Owned facility and equipment
- **Adaptability and Responsiveness:** Lean organizational structure allows for greater flexibility in meeting customer needs, as there are fewer protocols to navigate
- **Brand Positioning of Bread:**
  - Carefully handcrafted
  - Made from fresh, natural ingredients
  - Produced in a dairy and nut-free facility
  - Free of additives
  - Vegan-friendly
  - Offers higher nutritional value than competing brands

Context–External Barriers: Migration affects job stability at the bakery. Natural ingredients can be challenging to acquire, and protein prices are volatile

Context–External Enablers: The brand is well-known. The growing trend among millennials and Generation Z for allergen-free bread presents opportunities to increase the bread's visibility in supermarket chains

SNAPSHOT PART 3: LISTING AND CATEGORIZING PROCESS COMPONENTS

Your process is how you generate your products or services. For Mora and other manufacturing facilities, her process entails a supply chain. Her process encompasses all activities associated with the production and delivery of bread, shown in the straightforward cycle graphic in Figure 4.7, Part 3. She starts with purchasing raw materials (e.g., flour, yeast, eggs, and other ingredients) and finishes with distributing the bread to restaurants, national supermarket chains, and other local, non-national supermarkets).

Fig. 4.7. Listing Processes of Mora's Bakery

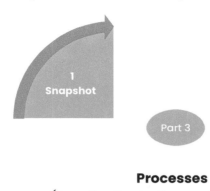

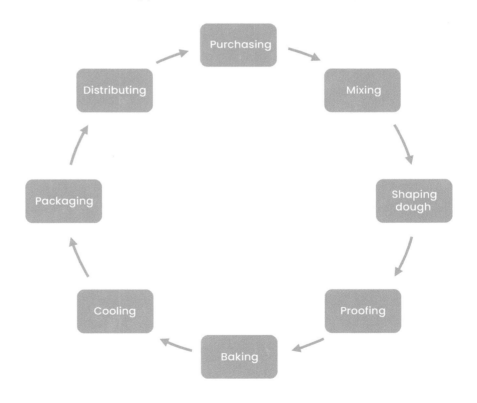

Processes
(Supplier, Production, and Distribution)

Unless you run a bakery like Mora, your diagram will look very different based on your industry. For example, if I were to document my process for studying the effectiveness of a training program, here is the list of steps I would use to model my process.

1. Define the objectives.
2. Develop a data collection (e.g., survey) and analysis plan (e.g., inferential statistics).
3. Obtain approval from the Institutional Review Board (IRB) to collect data from program participants.
4. Select the sample.
5. Administer the survey.
6. Monitor response rates.
7. Clean the data.
8. Analyze the data.
9. Interpret the results.
10. Report the findings.
11. Develop recommendations.
12. Disseminate the results and recommendations.
13. Encourage the use of findings to inform future program improvements, adjustments, or expansions.
14. Evaluate the need for further research or follow-up studies to continue monitoring the program's effectiveness over time.

Here is another example for a company that does commercial construction projects.

1. Do market research and opportunity identification.
2. Create business development and client acquisition.
3. Prepare project bid and submit a proposal.
4. Negotiate and sign a contract.
5. Plan and schedule the project.
6. Obtain permits and approvals.
7. Procure resources and management.
8. Prepare site and construction.
9. Initiate quality control and inspection.
10. Complete and hand over the project.
11. Provide post-construction support, such as warranty services, maintenance, and repairs, to ensure the client's ongoing satisfaction with the completed project.
12. Maintain relationships with clients for potential future projects and referrals.

Your process might be best expressed as a cycle like Mora's, or a linear model, from point A to point B. Yours may have more or fewer steps than Mora's or mine, depending on your business model. Regardless of how you express it, please take the opportunity to distill your process into a simple chart like the one in Figure 6. It clarifies what you do so you can evaluate it.

CATEGORIZE BARRIERS AND ENABLERS
(Snapshot 3.1 and 3.2)

In Figure 4.8, Parts 3.1 and 3.2, Mora describes her barriers and enablers again, but this time in relation to her process. By categorizing your processes as enablers and barriers, you better understand what is working well and what needs to be adjusted.

For your business or organization, categorize any processes that contribute to your company's efficiency and productivity as enablers. Categorize any processes that hinder progress or create bottlenecks as barriers. This part is critical for Step 2 of SEAM because it helps determine where and how to automate and introduce digital technologies to streamline your operations, improve performance, and ultimately boost your bottom line. It also lets us know if your business can effectively respond to changing market conditions and customer needs.

Mora finds the visual representation of the bakery's processes in Figure 4.8 very valuable in highlighting the importance of having work-flows for each step. This will enable her team to understand the interrelationships and dependencies between tasks involved in making and delivering bread. Also, in this final step, Mora completes the list of contextual factors that she started in the previous section. She is getting closer to determining the activities that will enable her transformation!

Fig. 4.8. Categorizing Bakery's Processes into Barriers or Enablers

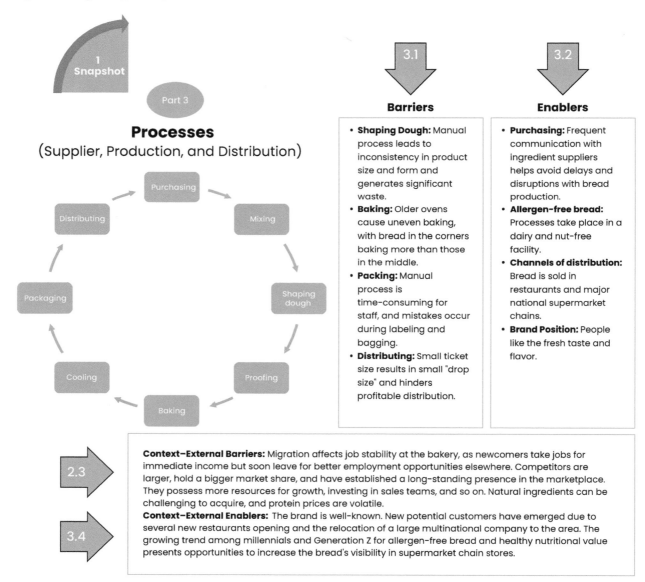

Part 3

Processes
(Supplier, Production, and Distribution)

1 Snapshot

Purchasing → Mixing → Shaping dough → Proofing → Baking → Cooling → Packaging → Distributing → Purchasing

3.1

Barriers

- **Shaping Dough:** Manual process leads to inconsistency in product size and form and generates significant waste.
- **Baking:** Older ovens cause uneven baking, with bread in the corners baking more than those in the middle.
- **Packing:** Manual process is time-consuming for staff, and mistakes occur during labeling and bagging.
- **Distributing:** Small ticket size results in small "drop size" and hinders profitable distribution.

3.2

Enablers

- **Purchasing:** Frequent communication with ingredient suppliers helps avoid delays and disruptions with bread production.
- **Allergen-free bread:** Processes take place in a dairy and nut-free facility.
- **Channels of distribution:** Bread is sold in restaurants and major national supermarket chains.
- **Brand Position:** People like the fresh taste and flavor.

2.3 **Context–External Barriers:** Migration affects job stability at the bakery, as newcomers take jobs for immediate income but soon leave for better employment opportunities elsewhere. Competitors are larger, hold a bigger market share, and have established a long-standing presence in the marketplace. They possess more resources for growth, investing in sales teams, and so on. Natural ingredients can be challenging to acquire, and protein prices are volatile.

3.4 **Context–External Enablers:** The brand is well-known. New potential customers have emerged due to several new restaurants opening and the relocation of a large multinational company to the area. The growing trend among millennials and Generation Z for allergen-free bread and healthy nutritional value presents opportunities to increase the bread's visibility in supermarket chain stores.

CONSIDERING THE OPTIONS

At the end of Step 1 of SEAM, Mora now has a holistic view of her business, examining both its barriers and enablers in terms of resources and processes. This analysis helps her to identify what may help or hinder the transformation of the bakery. She also can see the big picture of her business and the options that lie before her. She can even list and consider them individually, as many business owners do after they complete their Snapshot.

At this point, many business owners are surprised by what they discover. I've seen businesses head in a completely unexpected direction after completing their Snapshot step. What will Mora decide? She must consider the possibilities for herself and Mora's Bakery, and there are many!

1. *Stay and grow the business:* To achieve better outcomes, Mora needs to eliminate any barriers, as well as embrace automation and integrate technology into her bakery.
2. *Sell the company:* Fixing a business is hard work, and Mora has built an excellent asset to sell (e.g., her bread is in national supermarkets). Selling the bakery may be a painless exit strategy.
3. *Retain the status quo:* The Snapshot has revealed that sales will continue to drop without a substantial change in the business. If Mora does nothing, it may well mean the company's end.
4. *Become a co-packer:* Mora has an advantage because her bakery is dairy and nut free. She could bake bread for other companies as a co-packer. Her name would no longer be on the product, but she could retain her business and collaborate for greater success.
5. *Work with a co-packer:* Mora could hire a fully staffed, more modern bakery to produce her recipes. However, the facility would have to be dairy and nut free.
6. *Find a partner and scale up:* There are many options here. Mora could find an operational partner to take care of production while she concentrates on sales. Together they could obtain a loan from the U.S. Small Business Administration (SBA) to update her equipment and create an integrated system, aided by AI and IoT, where equipment automates processes and orders ingredients. They could even hire a

sales team for more overall growth. In another option, Mora could legally partner with a larger bakery and work as a team to promote the artisan bread. Or she could legally contract a smaller bakery to produce Mora's bread with a clear delineation of roles, profit-sharing, etc.

Mora has a lot to think about, and the next step of SEAM, the Envision step, will clarify her decision-making.

YOUR SNAPSHOT

When Mora approached my consulting company, Windrose Vision, she asked for specific strategies to increase her revenue by attracting more customers using social media. She was not thinking about examining her entire company's operations. Helping Mora create her Snapshot was our critical first step on her journey to digital transformation.

As you think about creating your own Snapshot, keep in mind that in the SEAM model, sales and marketing must respond to the quality and production value of the product or process itself. The product and process must be good for sales and marketing to succeed. In Spanish, we have a saying, "Nadie da lo que no tiene," or in English, "You can't get blood from

a stone." This means if the process is flawed and the product is inadequate, all the sales and marketing in the world will not help a business or organization reach its desired outcomes.

When we speak of transformation with SEAM, we strive to impact how a business or organization produces and delivers its products and services to meet a specific audience's needs. We also are examining whether a business can deliver as promised, how it can eliminate inefficiencies to maximize profit, and how it can create new and improved products and services.

Now that you have experienced creating a Snapshot in the SEAM model for Mora's business, we invite you to create your own! All the figures and blank templates are available in appendix 1 at the end of the book.

After you've completed the Snapshot, keep reading. Next, we'll put our imagination to work to uncover the "E" of the SEAM model—Envision.

Chapter 5

SEAM Step 2: ENVISION

"Dream and give yourself permission to envision a you that you can choose to be."

Joy Page

The second step of SEAM is the "E" or the Envision step. It's one of my favorite parts of the process because it summons the entrepreneurial spirit of my clients. Many of my clients say that the Snapshot model validated what was working and needed improvement in their business, but the Envision step helped them determine their best course of action.

The experience was similar for Mora. At the end of the Snapshot step, she considered the many options for her business, from transforming Mora's Bakery to selling it. Like many of my clients, Mora had an epiphany about her artisanal bread business. Despite her challenges and identified barriers to her desired outcomes, Mora's confidence in her product increased after taking inventory of her enablers. Her list of enablers showed that her bread had great potential with a broader audience of health-conscious consumers. She was hopeful she had a viable audience with consumers who appreciated the unique, flavorful bread made without additives, as well as those with allergies to nuts and dairy. This audience would also include individuals who prefer or require vegan bread.

Mora realized that she was not ready to sell. Instead, she would embrace the transformative journey of improving her bakery and expanding her artisanal bread offerings. By streamlining her operations and enhancing the customer experience, Mora can position her artisanal bread business as a more attractive investment opportunity. This not only prepares the business for a potential future sale, should she desire, but also helps ensure its long-term success.

To complete the Envision step, Mora must imagine how to grow and scale Mora's Bakery.

WHY ENVISION YOUR TRANSFORMATION JOURNEY?

Your journey will be completely different from Mora's journey. You may launch an e-commerce site or a consultancy instead of manufacturing a product. However, you and Mora share the entrepreneur experience.

Do you remember the first sale of your product or delivery of your service? Or the first time you heard the customer say, "This is what I was looking for!" It was so exciting to solve a customer problem; you made it happen because you had a vision with a purpose. It wasn't just about creating or doing something for your customers. It was about producing something that brought specific, desired value to the customer.

Reconnecting with that memory can prepare you for the Envision step, which has many benefits for your transformation:

ENVISION TURNS YOUR VISION FOR BUSINESS TRANSFORMATION INTO ACTION: The Envision step is motivating. By determining what you want to accomplish for your business or organization, you can align your resources, and efforts toward realizing your desired outcomes.

ENVISION HELPS YOU DETERMINE THE PATH FORWARD. THE ENVISION STEP IS A CATALYST: The Snapshot step may provide broad insight into your business or organization, but the research and process of Envision will give you the confidence to make the right decisions.

ENVISION PROVIDES MEASURABLE OUTCOMES: Envision helps you to focus. In the Envision step, you set specif-ic outcomes to work toward. These become benchmarks to help measure progress as you advance in your transformation.

MORA'S ENVISION STEP

As shown in Figure 1, Mora will use the bakery's Step 1 Snapshot as a starting point to visualize the transformation of her business in SEAM Step 2 Envision. She will begin by focusing on the customer (Part 1) and using what she learns to develop the bakery's impact statement (Part 2). From there, Mora will examine how to mitigate her barriers and decide where to automate and integrate digital technologies into her bakery (Part 3). Finally, she will reconsider her outcomes, KPIs, and strategies (Part 4), and think about her next five years (Part 5).

Fig. 5.1. SEAM Envision Step for Mora's Bakery

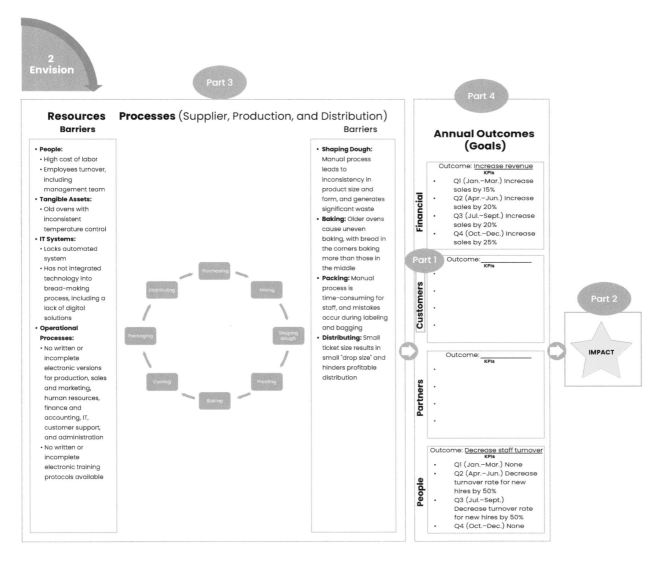

2 Envision

Part 3

Resources
Barriers

- **People:**
  - High cost of labor
  - Employees turnover, including management team
- **Tangible Assets:**
  - Old ovens with inconsistent temperature control
- **IT Systems:**
  - Lacks automated system
  - Has not integrated technology into bread-making process, including a lack of digital solutions
- **Operational Processes:**
  - No written or incomplete electronic versions for production, sales and marketing, human resources, finance and accounting, IT, customer support, and administration
  - No written or incomplete electronic training protocols available

Processes (Supplier, Production, and Distribution)
Barriers

Purchasing · Mixing · Shaping dough · Proofing · Baking · Cooling · Packaging · Distributing

- **Shaping Dough:** Manual process leads to inconsistency in product size and form, and generates significant waste
- **Baking:** Older ovens cause uneven baking, with bread in the corners baking more than those in the middle
- **Packing:** Manual process is time-consuming for staff, and mistakes occur during labeling and bagging
- **Distributing:** Small ticket size results in small "drop size" and hinders profitable distribution

Part 4

Annual Outcomes (Goals)

Financial

Outcome: <u>Increase revenue</u>
KPIs
- Q1 (Jan.–Mar.) Increase sales by 15%
- Q2 (Apr.–Jun.) Increase sales by 20%
- Q3 (Jul.–Sept.) Increase sales by 20%
- Q4 (Oct.–Dec.) Increase sales by 25%

Part 1

Customers

Outcome: _____
KPIs
-
-
-

Partners

Outcome: _____
KPIs
-
-

People

Outcome: <u>Decrease staff turnover</u>
KPIs
- Q1 (Jan.–Mar.) None
- Q2 (Apr.–Jun.) Decrease turnover rate for new hires by 50%
- Q3 (Jul.–Sept.) Decrease turnover rate for new hires by 50%
- Q4 (Oct.–Dec.) None

Part 2

IMPACT

ENVISION PART 1: TAKING THE PULSE OF YOUR CUSTOMER BASE

Any transformation of a business or organization should begin with thinking about the customer. Adopting a customer-centric approach prioritizes customers' needs, expectations, and behaviors. By understanding and prioritizing customers or target audience, SEAM users can improve their business or organization and create new products and services that effectively cater to a target audience.

That's why the first part of the Envision step in SEAM is to take the pulse of your customers. Within SEAM, doing so helps refine the customer outcomes you reported in your Snapshot or create new ones, but it also keeps you focused on who you serve. Mora did not

have any customer outcomes in her Snapshot, as shown in Figure 5.1, Part 1, but she will add them in the Envision step.

What methods does your business use to obtain customer insights? You can use surveys, focus groups, interviews, user testing, feedback forms, sales and customer service interactions, and market research to glean valuable customer information. Social media also has become a vital tool for understanding customer preferences, tracking trends, and fostering product development.

If you run a B2C business like a retail store or e-commerce site, social media is a highly effective tool for tracking customer preferences and nurturing emotional connections. It enables direct customer interaction to monitor their preferences and behaviors over time. Social media also provides a platform for feedback and caters to consumers' expectations for customization.

Mora's Bakery operates as B2B, catering to clients such as restaurants, national supermarket chains, and local, independent grocery stores. B2B businesses, like bakeries, may lack direct access to valuable consumer data about the end users of their products. Mora does not interact directly with customers who purchase her bread at the supermarket stores or those who dine at the restaurants who serve her bread. However, it's important to note that the supermarkets maintain records of purchase behavior related to her bread. As Mora embarks on her journey, she should keep this information in mind. Also, she should be open to adopting strategic approaches for social media, such as engaging with industry influencers, hosting virtual events, participating in industry discussions, and encouraging employee advocacy.

QUESTIONS TO TAKE THE PULSE OF YOUR CUSTOMERS

As you complete your own SEAM Envision step (shown in Figure 5.1, Part 1), you must respond to the questions below.

a. **Does your business primarily cater to B2B, B2C, or a mix of both?** *If B2B, please specify the types of businesses you serve. If B2C, provide a brief description of your target consumer demographics.*

b. **Does your business focus on addressing customers' needs"(requirements or de-** sires), **pain points (challenges, problems, or frustrations), or does it tackle both?** *This question helps you to evaluate your current strategy and to identify areas for improvement.*

c. **Have your customers' needs or pain points regarding your product remained consistent or changed since last year?** *Include data source. This question is valuable in understanding how your customers' needs and pain points are evolving and gives insight into how change would influence them.*

d. **What value does your product or service bring to the customer?** *Include your data source. This question helps you to identify the unique selling points, features, or qualities that set your product apart from competitors and make it valuable to the customers.*

e. **How satisfied are your customers with your products or services?** *Include your data source. This question helps you identify areas where your business excels, as well as areas that need improvement to enhance customer satisfaction.*

Mora did not draft customer outcomes in her annual business plan because she thought that producing healthy bread (her output) was enough to keep customers engaged. The SEAM Envision step challenges her to develop customer outcomes to strengthen the relationship between Mora's Bakery and their customers. She begins "taking the pulse of her customers" by reflecting on the questions above.

In this case, her only data source is anecdotal evidence, or comments she has received from customers and those who have tasted her bread. As you complete this step for your own purposes, you may have anecdotal evidence of your own, customer surveys, or even online comments and reviews that will help you to answer all the questions.

a. Mora's Bakery sells bread to other businesses (B2B). Customers include 1) national supermarket chains, 2) local, independent grocery stores, and 3) small and large restaurants.

b. Mora's bread is a fresh, premium product made of all-natural ingredients without preservatives. The products satisfy a want, not a need, because people could buy frozen or commercially produced bread with additives that provide a longer shelf life. However, Martha's Bakery products meet a specific need for those who have nut and dairy allergies, require a gluten-free diet, or prefer vegan food.

c. Mora sees increasing demand from small and large restaurants, especially from smaller restaurants that cater to younger clientele. The bread sales at supermarkets vary, depending on the store. It sells some months better than others. Since Mora's Bakery is a supplier to national chain supermarkets, she does not have access to their data about the characteristics of customers. Mora infers that the customers in specialty supermarkets are very health conscious.

Mora can support her answers with data from the American Baker's Association (ABA) Study: Attracting Millennial Customers. (Juhl 2019) The data says 73 percent of millennials buy bread, and 75 percent do not like wasting bread from large loaves. Also, 48 percent said they would try a product if the ingredients were responsibly sourced. Another report, Top 10 Predictions for Baked Goods Trends in 2022 (Ali 2022) showed consumers are embracing a trend toward artisanal bread baked in smaller loaves. People, especially millennials, would rather buy and consume a whole, smaller-sized loaf than purchase a larger one and discard uneaten bread. Another trend that will continue is vegan and gluten-free baking as more people become dairy, nut, and gluten intolerant.

d. Mora offers the following value to her customers. Her data source is anecdotal evidence from customers and those who know her products.

- **High-quality ingredients:** Mora bakes with natural, locally sourced, and organic ingredients, catering to the preferences of health-conscious customers.
- **Unique flavors and textures:** Mora's bread comes in various distinctive flavors, textures, and styles, providing customers with a unique and enjoyable eating experience.
- **Tradition:** Mora uses her aunt's techniques and recipes. Her customers appreciate tradition.
- **Freshness:** Mora's Bakery products are sold fresh, ensuring customers the best possible taste and quality.
- **Dietary restrictions:** Mora's bread is baked in an allergen-free facility, and a safe option for people with dairy and nut allergies and those who prefer vegan bread.

Mora has never conducted surveys or interviews with her customers to gauge their satisfaction with Mora's Bakery products, nor does she collect feedback on her website. However, the delivery staff has relayed positive comments from the restaurants.

Mora's research indicates that the bakery has a bright future because Gen Z, millennial, and health-conscious consumers are likely to continue buying her bread. Her higher-quality ingredients and slower fermentation times create a better texture for her bread. The premium quality, unchlorinated, and unbleached bread flour creates a desirable structure and ultra-fine smoothness while adding high protein content to her product, which is ideal for better-tasting sourdough. Mora feels her customers recognize and appreciate her bread's nutritional and vegan aspects. She insists on retaining the integrity of her products (and continuing to please her customers) as she transforms her bakery.

ENVISION PART 2: ARTICULATING THE IMPACT STATEMENT

Having taken the pulse of the customer, the next step for Mora is to articulate her impact statement. The key question is, "What positive change does the business or organization bring to society, nature, and the community in which it operates?"

When doing your own Envision step, taking the pulse of the customer equips you with valuable insights to refine or to help you create one. The impact statement should capture the broader aspirations of your organization and encompass its social, environmental, and economic contributions. If you prioritize the pulse of your customers, you will automatically shape your impact statement with an intuitive understanding of customer needs, expectations, and preferences. Synchronizing your customer insights and your organization's broader aspirations will build a robust foundation for sustainable growth.

Your impact statement also should be consistent with your corporate social responsibility (CSR) strategy. CSR has become a priority for businesses as today's consumers seek out companies that share their values and beliefs. (Cresanti 2019)

CSR can have powerful effects and build trust and brand loyalty with their customer base. Many large companies have dedicated CSR departments or teams, but the same benefits are available for small businesses and organizations. Small businesses and organizations impact their city and surrounding areas through job creation and services and active participation in civic events. A shopkeeper in the town center often receives integral, visible opportunities to regularly engage with the community by sponsoring a pee wee baseball league or donating to the local food pantry. (Cresanti 2019)

Because Mora is a manufacturer, she can directly impact society through her product. If she was outsourcing her manufacturing overseas, she might articulate a different impact statement based on her suppliers and their values. If you sell online or have another service business, you undoubtedly employ technology to work toward your goals within a customer service ecosystem. You may articulate your impact statement based on the ecosystem you use. For example, if you use Amazon as a service provider, does its business practices align with your impact statement?

Some companies overtly integrate their impact statement with their product. For example, a shoe manufacturer may donate shoes to the underprivileged when their sales reach a certain threshold, or a personal products manufacturer may support homeless shelters with toiletries, etc. How you articulate your impact statement is up to you, but it should always be authentic to your business or organization's values.

In this step, Mora solidifies her impact statement by answering the following questions:

a. **How do your business's or organization's CSR initiatives align with your company's vision?**
   The answer here will tell whether a business or organization exhibits actions in line with its values.

b. **How does your business or organization engage its employees in CSR initiatives?**
   Your employees may participate in your CSR efforts or maybe even lead them.

c. **How does your business or organization**

ensure that the CSR initiatives are genuine, rather than just for public relations purposes?
The answer to this question concerns public perception. Are your corporate activities being perceived as authentic?

Here is how Mora answered the questions:

a. Mora firmly believes that her products are intrinsically linked to her CSR and is deeply committed to this cause. She actively supports her community by participating in charity events and sponsoring local organizations, usually with donations of her bread products.

b. The bakery staff is responsible for organizing two community events a year, and they all understand her commitment to CSR.

c. Mora shows her commitment to CSR, not just public relations, but through her desire to certify as a B Corporation (B Corp) within the next five years. This certification is not required in any way. Still Mora desires the honorable third-party endorsement of her organization's commitment to high social and environmental performance, accountability, and transparency on many factors, including employee benefits, charitable giving, supply chain practices, and materials used in production. (bcorporation.net n.d.) Mora's Bakery is subject to a review process to become a B Corp. The bakery's performance is measured against set standards before it can be deemed worthy of certification and publicly listed with a B Corp profile. Mora also will make a legal commitment by changing the bakery's corporate governance structure to be more accountable to all stakeholders. (bcorporation.net n.d.)

Based on her answers to questions in Part 1 and Part 2, Mora is ready to write an impact statement for the bakery. Her impact statement will answer the question, "What positive change does the business or organization bring to society, nature, and the community in which it operates?"

Do you have a written impact statement for your business or organization? If not, think about the positive changes you hope your business brings about in society and try to articulate it within a few sentences. Your impact statement should inspire your employees and resonate with your customers. Use our answers to the questions in Part 1 to remind you what is important to your customers as you draft your statement. Also, make sure you describe what your business or organization is doing to achieve the changes you want. Here is Mora's impact statement:

Mora's Bakery strives to foster a healthier community and a sustainable future by producing nutritious, natural bread products, free from additives and specifically crafted to be allergen-free, while actively reducing waste and promoting sustainability in our operations.

ENVISION PART 3: OVERCOMING BARRIERS THROUGH DIGITAL TRANSFORMATION

SEAM helps business owners advocate for a targeted approach to digital transformation. We aim to address barriers in resources and processes that inhibit a business's or organization's ability to operate more efficiently and effectively and to adapt to changes quickly. It's essential to examine these barriers individually as well as in the context of their interrelationships.

It is critical to understand that digital transformation is a continuous journey rather than a fixed destination. As the landscape of technology evolves, so will the digital transformation of your business or organization. If you have a targeted approach to your transformation, your small business or organization can take incremental steps in the journey, building momentum to secure buy-in and support from stakeholders. By tackling critical areas and showcasing immediate benefits, any business or organization can lay the groundwork for an extensive, high-impact transformation. For a structured, purposeful approach to digital transformation, SEAM emphasizes seven key aspects: (Westerman, Bonnet, and McAfee 2014) (Siebel 2019)

1. *AUTOMATION:* Implementing technologies to streamline repetitive tasks and processes, which enhances efficiency and minimizes human error.
2. *DIGITIZATION:* Converting analog information and processes into digital formats for more accessible storage, analysis, and retrieval.
3. *DIGITALIZATION:* Utilizing digitized information and processes to streamline and automate tasks, enhancing efficiency and reducing costs.
4. *DATA ANALYTICS:* Harnessing data to make informed decisions, identify trends, and optimize operations.
5. *ENHANCED CUSTOMER EXPERIENCES:* Utilizing digital tools and channels to create seamless, personalized, and convenient customer interactions.
6. *NEW BUSINESS MODELS:* Innovating and adapting business models to leverage digital technologies and generate new revenue streams.
7. *CULTURAL CHANGE:* Cultivating an environment that embraces innovation, adaptability, and the effective implementation of new technologies and processes.

QUESTIONS TO EXAMINE BARRIERS

It is important to examine barriers because they are what stand between our present-day business or organization and our transformation to something better. Lifting or eliminating them begins with a clear examination of our process and where the barriers lie. This involves answering a series of questions to clarify the areas we must address, and then, which ones we should address first.

a. **What are the current trends in your industry concerning various aspects of digital transformation, such as automation,**

digitization, digitalization, data analytics, enhanced customer experiences, new business models, and cultural change?

The best way to answer this question is by researching the current trends in your industry. The answers you discover will inform your decision about where to invest your resources and which aspect of digital transformation is most crucial for staying competitive in the marketplace.

b. **How would you prioritize and address the barriers in light of their impact on your business and the digital technology trends in your industry?**

Consider the barriers individually, but also how they interact with each other. Then, you can minimize the risk of implementing too many changes at a time by prioritizing and addressing your most critical barriers.

c. **In what sequence would you purchase the required digital technology to address the identified critical barriers?**

The answer to this question will undoubtedly have to do with the estimated cost of your transformation. Technology requires a significant investment, and few businesses or organizations have the resources to finance

all their plans at once. Consider the impact of the barriers on your business or organization, and again prioritize changes that will maximize your resources and offer the most significant return on investment.

Mora answered the questions based on her research on the state of the bakeries and what she discovered by filling in Figure 2.

a. Mora sought and found examples of how other bakers were incorporating digital technology into their operation. Her research revealed a trend among artisanal bread bakeries. They were using digital technology to enhance the traditional bread-making process, from recipe development to the final product's sale.

The information inspired her to think about her own digital transformation.

- **Recipe management:** Digital recipe management systems help bakers to develop and store standardized recipes, streamline production, reduce errors, and improve the consistency of their products.
- **Automated production:** Automated equipment like mixers, ovens, slicers, and even robotics, improve the accu-

racy and consistency of artisanal bread production. They reduce waste and repetitive movements, so bakers save time and can focus on other aspects of their craft.

• **Quality control:** Digital sensors and monitoring systems help bakers maintain consistent quality by tracking temperature, humidity, and other factors.

•**Traceability:** Digital systems can provide ingredient traceability to efficiently manage quality issues and food safety risks.

• **Augmented reality (AR) and virtual reality (VR):** AR and VR technologies are used to create immersive training experiences to learn from expert bakers without sharing the same physical location.

Her research also revealed that bakeries are using data analytics and digital technology, discovering new business models, and fostering cultural change through digital transformation. For example, bakeries are using data analytics to collect and analyze sales data to better understand their customers and optimize production schedules, minimize waste and improve supply chain management. Data analytics help bakeries improve customer experience with user-friendly online ordering platforms, and efficient delivery service with real-time status updates. Bakeries also are leveraging digital technology to develop new business models, like subscription-based services or offering intricate and customized bread designs with the help of 3D printing. Finally, introducing technology helps bakeries foster cultural change by improving cross-training sessions on bakery equipment, technology best practices, and overall employee efficiency.

b. Mora must answer the question, **"How would you prioritize and address the barriers in light of their impact on your business and the digital technology trends in your industry?"** Mora analyzes her model, as shown in Figure 5.2, and prioritizes the barriers in resources, processes, and those that appear in both areas based on their importance (Parts 3.1-3.3).

Fig. 5.2. Barriers in Mora's Bakery

2 Envision

Part 3

Processes (Supplier, Production, and Distribution)

Resources
Barriers

3.3
- **People:**
  - High cost of labor
  - Employees turnover, including management team

3.3
- **Tangible Assets:**
  - Old ovens with inconsistent temperature control

3.2
- **IT Systems:**
  - Lacks automated system
  - Has not integrated technology into bread-making process, including a lack of digital solutions

3.1
- **Operational Processes:**
  - No written or incomplete electronic versions for production, sales and marketing, human resources, finance and accounting, IT, customer support, and administration
  - No written or incomplete electronic training protocols available

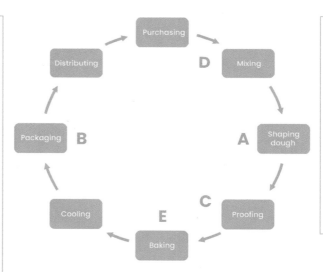

Barriers 3.3

- **Shaping Dough:** Manual process leads to inconsistency in product size and form, and generates significant waste
- **Baking:** Older ovens cause uneven baking, with bread in the corners baking more than those in the middle
- **Packing:** Manual process is time-consuming for staff, and mistakes occur during labeling and bagging
- **Distributing:** Small-ticket size results in small "drop size" and hinders profitable distribution

Barrier #1 (3.1) Operational Processes: Mora prioritizes the need to document her processes throughout the bakery's operations as shown in Figure 5.2, Resources, 3.1. Mora's incomplete electronic documentation of her processes affects almost all areas of the bakery. There is a corporate story that illustrates the importance of operational processes. In 2021, fast-food giant Burger King recruited one of the longtime executives from Domino's Pizza to troubleshoot their falling profit margins. The executive toured their franchise locations and discovered a critical flaw in the kitchen process. Sometimes, the employees were placing the cheese underneath the meat on some of the burgers, while at other times, they were putting it on top. The executive concluded that by standardizing the position of the cheese on the burgers, the employees could work more quickly and efficiently, thereby enhancing the customer experience. (Haddon 2022)

Had Burger King completed their SEAM model, they would have undoubtedly had a customer satisfaction outcome of increasing the accuracy of every customer's order. One of the barriers they would want to eliminate would be the delay in preparing their hamburgers due to the inconsistent processes (like how to add cheese to their burgers). Seconds accumulate into hours over time, and because burgers are made in an assembly line, if one individual does not correctly follow the procedure, it affects everyone. Standardizing the process, such as always placing the cheese on top of the burger, eliminates the barrier. This allows employees to assemble burgers faster, resulting in customers receiving their food more quickly.

Mora understands she needs to examine each of her operational processes, as outlined in the diagram in Figure 2. She also realizes that workflow maps will help employees understand the sequence of events within a task and make them feel like part of a team when they see how they fit into the overall process. Improving her operational processes will decrease ambiguity, boost productivity, and guarantee quality. Most importantly, Mora recognizes that standardizing her processes will help with staff turnover by correcting any weaknesses in her employee training. Bakery work is arduous, and bringing clarity to operational processes will help her create buy-in with employees and more easily hire and retrain staff.

Barrier #2 (3.2) IT Systems. Mora's second priority is to address her need for an IT system that integrates with her other processes (Figure 5.2, Resources, 3.2). Mora acknowledges that she needs a better IT solution within the bakery and wants to invest in an ERP system. She observes from her model how ERP would affect her entire process (Figure 5.2, Processes, 3.3). Her research revealed that ERP in bakeries significantly impacts three primary areas: production of goods, sales of products, and business administration. ERP software is an excellent solution for businesses and organizations, as it integrates various processes and functions. The software has the functionality to improve planning and scheduling, monitor inventory, and control costs in a multitude of ways. Mora is excited by the tremendous impact this tool could have on her bakery!

Also, Mora currently uses a Word document for traceability of her ingredients, which is inadequate and unacceptable for a bakery of her reach. Bakeries are responsible for addressing the complete traceability of incoming raw ingredients through the production, labeling, and packaging of baked goods. Experts agree that the results could be catastrophic if one of Mora's key ingredients was recalled and her traceability system was found deficient. (Smith 2020) By automating her traceability, Mora can track the receiving of raw materials, pre-scaling of minor ingredients, tracking of bulk ingredients and toppings, finished product labeling, and sales order fulfillment. Mora also learns that she has options when it comes to traceability technology. Even if she chooses an ERP that does not have built-in traceability, it is possible to add the functionality through third-party extensions or integrations.

She hopes to integrate inventory data across all areas of the bakery, allowing her to track ingredients, finished goods, and packaging materials in real time. The bakery can be optimized for peak performance. However, the ERP system must be compatible with the bakery's new equipment.

Barrier #3 (3.3): Tangible Assets and People. Mora's third priority concerns her equipment and the effect it has on her employees (Figure 5.2, Resources, 3.3 and Processes 3.3). She knows that having better equipment will increase her output. She also knows better equipment will make it easier for people to work for her and could consequently reduce turnover.

People would have to be specially trained on the new equipment, but it would still be easier for anyone working at the bakery to produce a more consistent, evenly baked, uniform product with little to no waste.

c. Mora must now answer the question, **"In what sequence would you purchase the required digital technology to address the identified critical barriers?"** This question is most pertinent to her processes (Figure 5.2, Processes, 3.3). She must consider the equipment she has and decide which of the units she should replace or install first.

1. *Shaping dough (A), controlling cost of goods by eliminating waste:* Mora has no control over the cost of her ingredients, but she can use them efficiently to control costs. She knows that her manual process in the Shaping Dough step leads to misshapen bread, inconsistent loaf sizes, and waste. Automating the process for shaping the dough would standardize the quality of her products. Integrating a dough divider with digital technologies, such as automated timers and sensors, will increase Mora's efficiency even more!

2. *Packaging (B), increasing efficiency and accuracy of labeling:* In Mora's Packaging step, the manual process of labeling and placing bread in bags often leads to errors, causing customers to receive incorrect items. By automating this process, she expects to fulfill orders faster, boosting the bakery's output. Also, with a new, digitally enabled packaging machine, especially if integrated with the ERP system, she can streamline inventory management because it automatically tracks the number of loaves of bread the bakery produces and packages.

3. *Proofing (C), standardizing the proofing process:* Currently, only Mora's head baker determines when the dough is done rising in the Proofing step. By automating the proofing, any trained bakery team member can supervise the process.

4. *Mixing (D), improving quality controls:* Mora recognizes that her older mixers may not mix ingredients uniformly, leading to variations in dough quality and finished products. A new mixer will consistently mix the ingredients and simplify the traceability process as the new ERP system integrates

real-time tracking, streamlines inventory management, and automates record-keeping.

5. ***Baking (E), reduce inconsistencies in baking:*** Mora recognizes that her ovens are old and have inconsistent heat distribution, leading to unevenly baked products and wasted energy. New ovens would work faster and more consistently than the older models. Also, AI and IoT-enabled equipment could help Mora monitor inventory and even place orders.

How can businesses effectively measure the potential returns on their invesment and weigh them against the associated costs? In response to this challenge, businesses and organizations often turn to cost-benefit analysis. This valuable tool allows them to evaluate and compare the potential costs and benefits associated with their investments, thereby enabling more informed decision-making.

Mora will use a cost-benefit analysis to determine whether investing in digital technologies for her bread-making operation is worthwhile. She will follow the same approach when procuring her ERP system to ensure sound decision-making. Here are some of the key steps she will take for her cost-benefit analysis. (Boardman 2017) (Berman 2018) You can take the same steps to determine how to proceed with your digital transformation, too.

1. Identify the costs: Mora must research the cost of equipment or, in the case of ERP, the software. All costs should be included in the estimate, including maintenance, installation costs or, in the case of software, the required license, hardware and infrastructure, implementation and customization, training, and ongoing support.

2. Identify the benefits: Increasing efficiency and productivity, improving decision-making, having better visibility into business operations, and increasing customer satisfaction are all reasons for Mora to procure new equipment and software.

3. Estimate the financial impact: This includes a calculation of the probable ROI, payback period, and net present value (NPV) of the investment.

4. Conduct a risk analysis: Mora must

consider all potential risks and uncertainties associated with upgrading her equipment and installing an ERP system, such as implementation delays, cost overruns, and resistance to change in her staff.

5. **Compare alternatives:** Mora also should shop around and compare costs and benefits of different solutions. For some entrepreneurs, this step involves weighing the advantages of upgrading versus buying a new product or software.

When it's time to invest in digital technologies for your operation, be sure to involve key stakeholders from your business or organization in the decision-making process. Seek advice from IT professionals, finance experts, and specialists in the specific digital technologies you want to purchase. Then you will surely address all perspectives and concerns. When Mora conducted her comprehensive cost-benefit analysis, she was confident her investment would profitably overcome her barriers to growth.

Having completed her cost-benefit analysis, Mora can now label the areas of desired automation within her process from A to D in the order she wants to prioritize her transformation.

DIGITAL TRANSFORMATION OUTCOMES

Your work in the Envision step will help you determine what part of your organization or business transformation you will complete in SEAM Year 1 and 2. Mora's SEAM Year 1 will be busy as she secures financing to purchase the ERP system and two new pieces of equipment: a dough shaper and packaging machine. Her two process-oriented outcomes by the end of SEAM Year 1 are: 1) installing, setting up, and integrating the ERP and the new equipment in the bakery's operations; and 2) providing comprehensive training to the bakery's team on these tools.

By the end of SEAM Year 2, Mora expects the purchases will have a return on investment by reducing labor costs and improving efficiency thereby boosting the bakery's financial performance. The ERP system will help her streamline her financial data which is now in several Excel sheets. A dough shaper will provide uniformity in the shape and appearance of the bread, reduce waste, and increase production. A bread packing machine will increase packaging speed and reduce errors.

ENVISION PART 4: EXAMINING OUTCOMES, KPI'S, AND STRATEGIES

In SEAM, the seven key aspects of digital technology—automation, digitization, digitalization, data analytics, enhanced customer experiences, new business models, and cultural change—should contribute to achieving the four specific types of outcomes of financial, customer, partners, and people. Mora will keep this in mind as she revisits the annual outcomes, KPIs, and strategies she initially established for the bakery in her Snapshot.

She must determine whether to maintain, eliminate, or refine them, taking into account the digital transformation initiatives she is planning through her work in Envision. This reevaluation ensures that her business strategies and transformation initiatives align and complement one another, setting her bakery up for success.

Let's examine how Mora reviews her existing outcomes and develops new ones more suitable to her evolving situation.

FINANCIAL OUTCOME

As shown in Figure 5.3, Mora reviewed the bakery's financial outcome for the year and decided to keep it.

She will devise a segmented marketing strategy to expand her customer base and achieve her financial outcome. Her plan is to focus on her millennial, Generation Z, health conscious, and environmentally concerned audience members. She aims to reach these demographics more effectively by contracting one of the national supermarket chains to engage them directly.

Figure 5.3 shows that Mora has stricken her idea of selling directly to consumers from her annual plan. She made this decision because her current business model does not support direct sales to consumers. Also, Mora sees that her brand is already in supermarkets and can expand there instead of completely changing her business model. Note that she has developed a strategy and corresponding activities specifically designed to target and expand into the upcoming establishments in the restaurant sector.

Fig. 5.3. Revised Strategies to Reach Financial Outcome

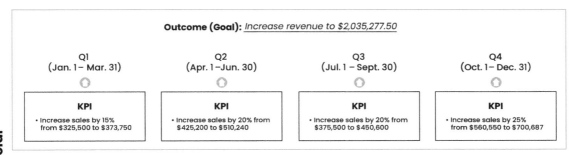

Financial

Outcome (Goal): *Increase revenue to $2,035,277.50*

Q1 (Jan. 1– Mar. 31)	Q2 (Apr. 1–Jun. 30)	Q3 (Jul. 1 – Sept. 30)	Q4 (Oct. 1– Dec. 31)
KPI • Increase sales by 15% from $325,500 to $373,750	**KPI** • Increase sales by 20% from $425,200 to $510,240	**KPI** • Increase sales by 20% from $375,500 to $450,600	**KPI** • Increase sales by 25% from $560,550 to $700,687

Strategy for Supermarkets: Develop a targeted marketing campaign using customer segmentation techniques. These techniques should consider factors such as lifestyle, purchasing habits, demographics, geographic locations, and specific nutritional requirements, such as the need for non-dairy and nut-free products.

Activities:
- Contract the digital marketing services of a national supermarket chain to design, plan, and implement a campaign targeting specific groups of consumers.
- Use existing relationships with national supermarket chains to expand into additional locations within the same chain.

Strategy for Restaurants: Highlight the health benefits and environmental impact of vegan, non-dairy, and nut-free bread products.

Activities:
- Offer tailored menu suggestions and recipes to the restaurants recently opened near the new headquarters of the large multinational company.
- Organize tasting events where restaurant owners and chefs can sample various artisanal breads, showcasing the bread's quality, flavor, and versatility as an accompaniment to their menu offerings.

CUSTOMER OUTCOME

For this outcome, Mora decides to focus on the restaurants to which she sells her bread. Mora currently monitors her service to ensure that her bread is delivered fresh and on time. Still, she has not yet formally collected the impressions of the restaurant owners or chefs about her products. She has anecdotal evidence from her delivery staff. For example, restaurant managers have told her delivery people, "No other bread compares to the smell and taste of Mora's freshly baked bread," and "We like the crispy texture on the outside and the soft, fluffy inside."

As outlined in Figure 5.4, Mora has identified many steps to learn about her restaurant customers' needs and expectations, such as finding the appropriate method to collect the data, deciding who she should get the data from, and developing a way to analyze the data. Once she accomplishes these steps, she will have a better understanding of the strategy she needs to market to her restaurant customers.

Fig. 5.4. New Customer Outcome, KPIs, and Strategies

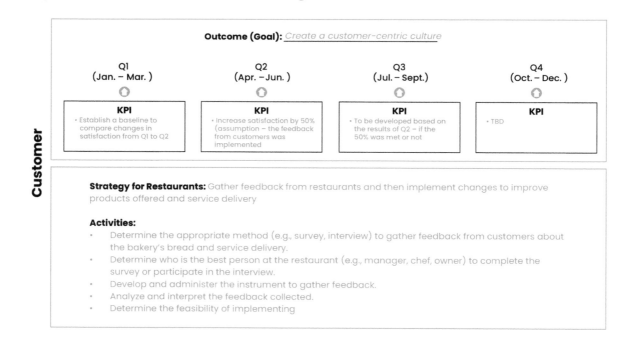

PARTNER OUTCOME

In Figure 5.5, Mora has set a Partner outcome to help her grow her business. She realizes that it is important to prioritize relationships with other bakeries, especially artisanal, vegan, and nut-free ones. Her strategy is to strengthen existing partnerships and build new ones. She hopes to expand her ecosystem of partners by formalizing her verbal agreements with other bakeries.

She sees through her SEAM work that automating and integrating digital technologies at the bakery would create extra time to devote to co-packing for another operation. Whether or not she goes the co-packer route, it will be advantageous for her to identify the purpose of all of her partnerships before and after the digital transformation

Fig. 5.5. New Partner Outcome, KPIs and Strategies

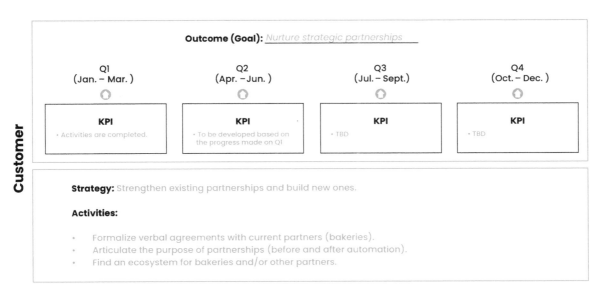

Outcome (Goal): *Nurture strategic partnerships*

Q1 (Jan. – Mar.)	Q2 (Apr. – Jun.)	Q3 (Jul. – Sept.)	Q4 (Oct. – Dec.)
KPI · Activities are completed.	**KPI** · To be developed based on the progress made on Q1	**KPI** · TBD	**KPI** · TBD

Customer

Strategy: Strengthen existing partnerships and build new ones.

Activities:

- Formalize verbal agreements with current partners (bakeries).
- Articulate the purpose of partnerships (before and after automation).
- Find an ecosystem for bakeries and/or other partners.

PEOPLE OUTCOME

As depicted in Figure 5.6, Mora has substituted "Decrease staff turnover" with "Foster ownership of the work among staff." This decision is grounded in her research on the latest trends in the industry. It emphasizes that maintaining employee engagement is a crucial aspect of retention.

In her research, Mora also learned about the principles of self-organizing teams and intends to apply them to the bakery with some modifications. The notion of "self-organizing teams" stems from the Scrum Agile framework, marked by a non-hierarchical structure. (Schwaber and Sutherland 2020) While management is responsible for assembling teams and defining goals and processes, teams are empowered to operate in a manner that best eliminates obstacles and barriers (Cross, Gardner, and Crocker 2021) They have autonomy, and the manager becomes more of a facilitator.

Mora wishes to grant her team autonomy. However, her priority to refine, to improve, and to complete standard operating procedures (SOPs) and workflows for each step of her processes suggests a more structured and centralized approach to organizing work.

Mora can achieve a balance by implementing SOPs and workflows, introducing flexible work shifts, promoting role rotation, and fostering a culture of peer-to-peer learning. With flexible work shifts, her team can self-organize their schedules, taking into account order volume and individual availability. Team members will be encouraged to rotate through various roles, such as baking and packaging, to develop a well-rounded skill set. By emphasizing peer-to-peer learning, Mora can create an environment where team members actively learn from one another's experiences. This approach enables self-organizing teams to adapt and enhance their performance based on their specific needs and collective knowledge.

Note that the KPIs in Figure 5.6 are process-oriented (whether completed or not) and unrelated to the performance of the staff (behavior change). Additional training will be given to staff after all the new equipment arrives and automation begins.

Also, notice that two strategies were scratched because there is only anecdotal data to support them. Mora decided that they also would be labor intensive (visiting the locations, establishing relationships, identifying liability, etc.) and take too long to become a reality.

Fig. 5.6. Revised People Outcome, KPIs, and Strategies

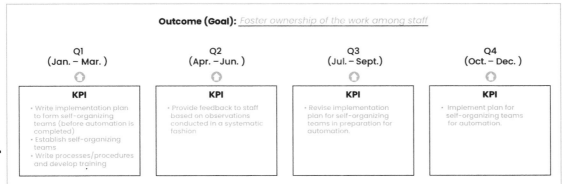

Outcome (Goal): _Foster ownership of the work among staff_

Q1 (Jan. – Mar.)	Q2 (Apr. –Jun.)	Q3 (Jul. – Sept.)	Q4 (Oct. – Dec.)
KPI	**KPI**	**KPI**	**KPI**
• Write implementation plan to form self-organizing teams (before automation is completed) • Establish self-organizing teams • Write processes/procedures and develop training	• Provide feedback to staff based on observations conducted in a systematic fashion	• Revise implementation plan for self-organizing teams in preparation for automation.	• Implement plan for self-organizing teams for automation.

People

Strategy: Apply elements of Agile methodology

Activities:
- Implement self-organizing teams

Strategy: Institute a peer-to-peer recruitment initiative

Activities:
- Provide incentives for staff who bring in additional personnel to work at the bakery.

ENVISION PART 5: MAPPING THE FUTURE

Figure 7 depicts Mora's ideas for a five-year journey to transform her bakery. As you prepare your own five-year plan, always remember that digital transformation is a journey, and the reality of your integration may not match your expected timing. As you transform your business, you must continue to operate as normal. Sometimes this means you will not progress with your digital transformation as quickly as you would like. Mora discovers this too!

Mora is off to a good start in SEAM Year 1 as she has already outlined the bakery's business outcomes, KPIs, and strategies in Part 4 of the Envision step. By the end of SEAM Year 1, she anticipates that her production will be transformed with the installation of the new ERP system. She also expects the new dough shaping and packaging equipment to be installed and training on the new technology will be underway. To fund the changes, she plans to either apply for a SBA loan or go to her bank. Her rapport with the bank is robust and her credit is excellent so she is confident she will secure a loan.

By the end of SEAM Year 2, Mora expects to see measurable changes, such as reduced labor costs, increased efficiency, and reduced waste. She expects this because of the dough shaper and packaging equipment. She also hopes to see better productivity across the bakery because of the new autonomy of the team. She also hopes to increase customer satisfaction through her new technologies and processes and use the ERP system to improve her accounting processes.

In SEAM Year 3, Mora intends to refine the bakery's processes further, and possibly even purchase new equipment or implement new technology to help her with automating some of the other parts of her process as identified in Figure 2, Process C and D, i.e., proofing and mixing. She anticipates the bakery will have greater quality control by Year 3, thanks to the ERP system's traceability capabilities and boosted by new health and safety initiatives and a greater sense of ownership among the team. In SEAM Year 3, Mora also expects to seriously begin working towards her B Corp status which remains an ambition for her.

By Year 4, Mora expects to reevaluate the business options before her, including the opportunity to partner with another bakery or become a co-packer. Her digital transformation in progress will support either of these goals and make her a desirable collaborator.

If Mora chooses or creates a new business model in Year 4, by Year 5, she expects to be testing it. She also expects to be operating under her new identity as a B Corp, after spend-

ing two years completing the requirements for the new status.

Along with her five-year plan, Figure 5.7 also includes an auxiliary chart to track the seven aspects of digital transformation. Mora has filled out the chart with her expected year-to-year progress within each category.

Fig. 5.7 Five-Year Plan for Transformation

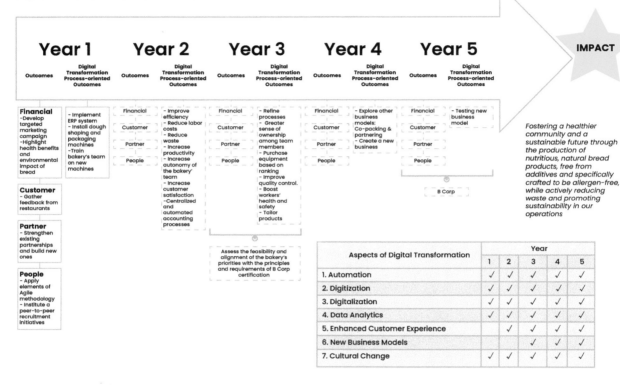

Year 1		Year 2		Year 3		Year 4		Year 5			IMPACT
Outcomes	Digital Transformation Process-oriented Outcomes	Outcomes	Digital Transformation Process-oriented Outcomes	Outcomes	Digital Transformation Process-oriented Outcomes	Outcomes	Digital Transformation Process-oriented Outcomes	Outcomes	Digital Transformation Process-oriented Outcomes		

Financial
-Develop targeted marketing campaign
-Highlight health benefits and environmental impact of bread

- Implement ERP system
- Install dough shaping and packaging machines
-Train bakery's team on new machines

Customer
- Gather feedback from restaurants

Partner
- Strengthen existing partnerships and build new ones

People
- Apply elements of Agile methodology
- Institute a peer-to-peer recruitment initiatives

Financial / Customer / Partner / People

- Improve efficiency
- Reduce labor costs
- Reduce waste
- Increase productivity
- Increase autonomy of the bakery' team
- Increase customer satisfaction
-Centralized and automated accounting processes

Financial / Customer / Partner / People

- Refine processes
- Greater sense of ownership among team members
- Purchase equipment based on ranking
- Improve quality control.
- Boost workers' health and safety
- Tailor products

Assess the feasibility and alignment of the bakery's priorities with the principles and requirements of B Corp certification

Financial / Customer / Partner / People

- Explore other business models: Co-packing & partnering
- Create a new business

Financial / Customer / Partner / People

- Testing new business model

B Corp

Fostering a healthier community and a sustainable future through the production of nutritious, natural bread products, free from additives and specifically crafted to be allergen-free, while actively reducing waste and promoting sustainability in our operations

Aspects of Digital Transformation	Year				
	1	2	3	4	5
1. Automation	✓	✓	✓	✓	✓
2. Digitization	✓	✓	✓	✓	✓
3. Digitalization	✓	✓	✓	✓	✓
4. Data Analytics	✓	✓	✓	✓	✓
5. Enhanced Customer Experience		✓	✓	✓	✓
6. New Business Models			✓	✓	✓
7. Cultural Change	✓	✓	✓	✓	✓

Mora has envisioned a transformation for her bakery and the strategies to get her there. However, each strategy must now be thought out before attempting execution. Even if Mora plans to hire a consultant or marketing firm to help her reach her outcomes, her work with SEAM will help her clearly express her needs to the consultant.

Next up is one of the most exciting steps in SEAM—the A, which stands for ACT! In the Act step, Mora will outline the actions she will take to achieve her outcomes, which will involve a return to our old friend—the logic model.

Have you determined the long-term outcomes for your business or organization? We encourage you to create your own! All the figures and blank templates are available in appendix 1 at the end of the book. If you use the SEAM framework, it will not only help you achieve your business and organizational outcomes, but also move you closer to making a significant impact on your community, and potentially, the world.

Chapter 6

SEAM Step 3: ACT

"A dream written down with a date becomes a goal. A goal broken down into steps becomes a plan. A plan backed by action makes your dreams come true."

Greg S. Reid

The third step of SEAM is the "A" or the Act. Action is necessary to move forward. Action serves as a catalyst for change and growth, propelling an organization towards its desired outcomes. It is like the yeast in Mora's bread recipes. Just as yeast changes the bread dough by making it rise to produce a light, fluffy loaf of bread, action produces the small changes that eventually result in the outcome you want to see. Different loaves of bread require different amounts of yeast, just as every outcome requires a specific action.

CONSEQUENCES OF THE ACT STEP

The Act step of SEAM can facilitate a dynamic process of discovery, learning, and professional growth.

DISCOVERY: Occurs as Mora identifies tasks to address the barriers and challenges in her processes. She might even discover solutions that she missed in the Envision step, which can help refine her plan and reach her outcomes sooner.

PROFESSIONAL GROWTH: A natural outcome of Mora's interaction with other bakers and sales teams, as they provide innovative solutions. She will strengthen her leadership skills as she effectively oversees the reskilling and upskilling of the bakery's team to adapt to the new technology.

LEARNING: Happens as Mora follows her plan and determines what works for the bakery and what must be adjusted. In fact, one of the biggest lessons Mora will learn is that adjusting her plan is normal and necessary to lift barriers as efficiently as possible. She will acquire knowledge and skills in a variety of software programs and systems, which will help her stay competitive and innovative in an ever-evolving digital landscape.

Mora is well prepared to act, but there is one more thing she needs—a solid action plan. An action plan is necessary to guide your actions as you implement what you envisioned in Chapter 5, even if you need to change and adapt the plan during implementation.

ACTING WITH FLEXIBILITY

When I worked at the NIH campus in

Bethesda, Maryland, I was known for my signature "walking meetings" with my team members. NIH is as large as a university campus, with various institutes and centers housed in different buildings. Walking from one building to another could take twenty minutes or more, so I would use the time to meet with my team members to develop strategies and task lists. Often, these meetings involved creating a divergent strategy about something because our original plan had become unworkable.

Back then, our directives often trickled down from the Office of Management and Budget at the White House to the Department of Health and Human Services, to the director of NIH, and ultimately, to my team to furnish updates on research for various health related nationwide initiatives. We were charged with pulling together the studies and contributions from various institutes. We had to hunt down the scientists in charge of a program or the one person in the institute who could answer our question. As you can imagine, these key players may or may not have been able to provide the information we needed to meet our deadlines and present updates. We had to have a Plan B in place because the NIH director was awaiting our response. In other words, despite our most meticulous planning, we often need-

ed to create a new strategy to provide everything we could by our rigorous deadline.

My team always remained focused on our specific outcome of delivering research updates on time; however, we also realized that even our Plan A would change if we received new information from any of the institutes at any time. We stayed flexible and responsive and rode the ebb and flow of strategy as it evolved and changed.

My experience is similar to the experience you will have in the Act step of SEAM. Even after all your hard work envisioning your strategies, your original plan may evolve with new information and activity, and that's okay. The ultimate plan has been tweaked and adjusted based on further details. However, every action begins with an initial action plan outlining a specific strategy. That is where Mora must start as well.

TIPS FOR TAKING ACTION

What do you need to know before taking action? Plenty. But before we discuss specifics, here are some tips for smoothly implementing your action plan regardless of your industry or action items.

RECORD YOUR INTENDED ACTIONS: In my experience, if it's not written, it won't happen. Ensure you transfer all the tasks you scribble on cocktail napkins or type into meeting minutes into your master action plan. Mora's work in the Envision step was a prelude to the Act step, where she continued to add and edit her task list as the plan unfolded. When in doubt, write it out. It's dangerous to rely on memory to recall the details and decisions discussed in every meeting.

FOSTER ACCOUNTABILITY AND OWNERSHIP: The action plan you develop in your Act step should be grounded in deadlines and assignments. All team members will be accountable for specific, assigned tasks. If your team is unaccustomed to strict deadlines or specific responsibilities, create opportunities for them to adapt. Allocate time in every meeting to address any concerns or challenges they have. Maintain an open-door policy and encourage open communication about their progress. Expect to clearly explain the purpose of the action plan to eliminate ambiguity about everyone's role in the project. By showing the connections among tasks, team members can see how their contributions fit into the larger picture.

BREAKING DOWN THE PLAN FOR EASIER EXECUTION: If implementing your action plan seems overwhelming, consider breaking it down into phases or sections. Doing so can make the entire project more easily achievable and manageable. For example, Mora broke her action plan into two sections: one to reach her annual business outcomes (financial, customer, partners, and people) and another for her transformation initiatives. Everything became (and was!) much easier to achieve.

COMPOSITION OF THE IMPLEMENTATION TEAM: In large businesses and organizations, there is often a dedicated team responsible for implementing an action plan for digital transformation. In smaller businesses and organizations, one or two people typically do the heavy lifting on implementing the action plan and assign smaller tasks to others. Whatever the size of your business or organization, the implementation team should have a detail-oriented member, who has a knack for keeping people on schedule and is responsible for tracking tasks from start to finish. As a consultant, I often work with such project managers to keep the team accountable, and to review and tweak strategies as the implementation unfolds.

However, it all starts with your first simple action, dictated by a strategy.

MORA'S ACT STEP

In her Act step, Mora will develop a comprehensive action plan based on her work in the Envision step. In the Envision step, Mora outlined activities for five years. In each of those years, her action plan will be divided into two sections as she executes her plan. The first section outlines the actions to achieve the bakery's business outcomes—financial, customers, partners, and people—while the second section details the steps to tackle the barriers to growth with digital technology.

As Mora develops her plan, she must consider the interplay between the bakery's operations and her efforts to transform it. For example, Mora will have to keep up bread production in the bakery during the installation of the new equipment. She may need to schedule workers to come in during off-times to make room for the installation during working hours. If Mora has thought through all the action items in her plan, she will be prepared to fill odd shifts in the bakery. Having a detailed action plan is essential for managing the chaos.

Mora also must be realistic about her timeline and the deadlines she sets. The speed at which she can implement changes depends on her own business, the schedule of her vendors, and the availability of equipment, among other factors. As you develop your action plan, remember that deadlines matter. Even more important, execute tasks correctly and do not rush through them.

To illustrate the development and execution of Mora's first section of her action plan, we will concentrate on one specific financial outcome strategy—the targeted marketing campaign. For the second section, we will focus on the first barrier Mora identified in Envision Part 3: the absence or incompleteness of bakery operational processes, either in written or electronic form, as well as the lack of or incomplete written or electronic training protocols.

SEAM STEP 3: ACT

PART 1: Establishing Before and After Action Review Meetings
PART 2: Choosing a Planning Tool
PART 3: Executing the Action Plan

ACT PART 1: ESTABLISHING BEFORE AND AFTER REVIEW MEETINGS

The foundation of a well-done action plan relies on a review process that evaluates progress, identifies bottlenecks and areas for improvement, detects deviations, and enables quick adjustments. This process fosters a culture of learning and adaptability, enabling effective responses to market shifts and emerging challenges. When it comes to planning and evaluating actions, few entities have a more finely honed protocol than the U.S. Army's Opposing Force (OPFOR).

The key to OPFOR's success is the Before-Action Review (BAR) and the After-Action Review (AAR). Before you act, holding a BAR meeting will help you to set expectations and to clearly define what the team expects to achieve. (Darling, Parry, and Moore 2005) The BAR allows team members to set their expectations, unify their approach, and prepare to meet expected challenges.

BAR meetings typically focus on answering four specific questions: (Darling, Parry, and Moore 2005)

- What is the expected result and measurement of the action?

- What challenges stand in our way?

- What have we learned from other situations?

- This time, what will make it successful?

While in AAR meetings, OPFOR develops future strategies based on past triumphs and failures. Following a military operation, OPFOR examines the outcomes they expected to achieve and to analyze what worked and what didn't. Then, OPFOR actively incorporates what they've learned in their next strategy rather than simply documenting the conclusions in a binder somewhere. Then, based on the past, OPFOR can develop a logical hypothesis: "Because x occurred in this mission, if we take action y next time, z will occur." Following this process, the AAR allows OPFOR to continuously improve and accurately predict how to strengthen the force's performance in the future. (Darling, Parry, and Moore 2005)

In an OPFOR post-military campaign AAR meeting, they typically consider the answers to four significant questions (Darling, Parry, and Moore 2005):

- What were our intended results?
- What were our actual results?
- What caused our results?
- What will we sustain or improve?

The answers to these questions help OP-FOR understand each mission's success (or lack thereof) and whether the same action should be sustained or improved. The AAR has been a part of military strategy since 1981 and has become a living, breathing part of OPFOR. It also has inspired the business world to adopt the concept.

Often, organizations only use OPFOR-style AAR meetings to evaluate the results they achieve for each strategy outlined in their action plan. However, it's even more effective to hold a BAR at the start of an activity (consisting of several tasks) and an AAR at the conclusion of all the tasks. You will create a feedback loop between thinking and action to move you purposefully toward your desired outcome. (Darling, Parry, and Moore 2005)

How will Mora leverage the BAR and AAR meetings?

These meetings are crucial for the successful planning and execution of her action plan. Mora will convene BAR meetings prior to undertaking activities or tasks, depending on their complexity. These meetings will provide a platform to monitor progress against the established timeline, purpose, and desired outcomes.

Once the activities are completed, AAR meetings will be held to reflect on the execution and to make necessary adjustments to the action plan and timeline. By implementing this iterative process of planning and reviewing, Mora ensures constant alignment and adaptation to achieve her business and digital transformation outcomes.

ACT PART 1: CHOOSING A PLANNING TOOL

A project management tool is a crucial component for effectively organizing, planning, and executing tasks within a team. There are hundreds of software tools, platforms, and frameworks to help you track and monitor your progress toward your outcomes. Microsoft Office 365 offers various productivity tools, while project management platforms (like Monday, Basecamp, and Asana) provide more specialized solutions. Each of them has pros and cons. Some are more visual than others; many have advanced integrations with other software programs and platforms that can streamline operations. Any of them will keep your team organized, connected, and appraised of progress on every phase of your implementation.

Which one is right for you? I don't necessarily advocate one tool over the other because your selection should be based on the specific needs of your business or organization, your team, and the project's complexity.

Most project management tools facilitate the listing, performance monitoring, and progress tracking of the following elements:

- Task description
- Name of the responsible person or team
- Completion due date
- Resources required
- Key milestones

There is no one-size-fits-all project management tool. However, here are a few considerations and suggestions to consider during the selection process.

Determine if and how to use the cloud: One specific decision you need to make is whether you will store your project management data on the cloud or an in-house server.

When I founded Windrose Vision, Office 365 was new. Everyone encouraged me to buy a reliable server rather than trust the cloud, but I appreciated the ease, accessibility, and shareability of the Office suite and still do! Now, Microsoft 365 includes collaboration tools, AI, and advanced security features. With the pandemic and the increase in remote workers on our team, Windrose is now wholly cloud based. My team can access everything they need from any computer with a login. Other businesses and organizations don't require such functionality. Adopt what works best for your organization.

Evaluate essential features: List the essential features you require, such as task management, collaboration tools, resource allocation, and reporting capabilities. Assess how each feature fits into your plan and contributes to your project management goals. Opt for a tool that offers a trial or demo period so your team can test its usability and determine if it's a good fit.

Focus on scalability and flexibility: Select a planning tool that can scale with your organization as your projects and teams grow. Ensure the tool is flexible enough to handle various project types, sizes, and complexities without compromising the essential features you identified in the above suggestions. Look for options—such as custom workflows, templates, and reporting features—that can help you tailor the tool to your organization's unique processes and preferences. Choose a tool that offers robust support and regular updates to keep up with industry standards and advancements.

Train everyone well: Whatever project management tool you choose, train the team together if possible and make the training sessions robust and comprehensive. When employees learn how to use project management tools from YouTube videos, they usually need additional guidance to put the tool into practice for their daily work. In other words, if you or your staff attempt to oversimplify or shortcut training on working with your project management tool, it will undoubtedly result in mistakes down the road.

Resist the temptation to revert: As you begin using your new planning tool, your team may become frustrated and clamor to return to their "old, comfortable way" of doing things, like using Excel. They may even become convinced that the old way is superior. Believe in your planning tool and stay the course! Automation can potentially enhance an organization's adaptability to future changes, and concurrently, yield time and cost savings.

MORA'S PLANNING TOOL

Mora chose Project for the web, Microsoft's product for cloud-based work and project management. It's an ideal choice because the execution of some tasks requires the completion of different tasks, and changes in one task may affect others. In addition, Mora's Bakery's transformation plan needed a visual timeline, such as Gantt chart for scheduling deadlines and showing task "dependencies," which Project for the web provides. These planning tools will be critical for her team to prepare for upcoming tasks and prevent bottlenecks.

In addition, Microsoft Project on the web includes a range of financial tools to monitor expenses, revenue, and other financial metrics so Mora can input her financial goals and KPIs; however, she does not know yet if she wants to use that functionality.

Let's refer to Figure 6.1, which demonstrates how Mora used her project management tool to efficiently plan her strategy to achieve the bakery's financial outcome. Mora breaks down the strategy into activities and then manageable tasks. She assigns roles and responsibilities to her team members. The tool allows her to create a clear timeline for completion, set deadlines, and track progress. Mora can collaborate with her team members, share updates, and adjust in real-time. Most importantly, she can monitor progress with the tool's tracking and reporting.

Action Plan Section 1: Bakery's SEAM Business Outcomes for Year 1	
Outcome Category: Financial	
Outcome: Increase revenue	
Period: Q3	
KPI: Increase sales by 20 percent	

Strategy: Develop a targeted marketing campaign using customer segmentation techniques. These techniques should consider factors such as lifestyle, purchasing habits, demographics, geographic locations, and specific nutritional requirements, such as the need for non-dairy and nut-free products.

Activity: Contract the digital marketing services of a national supermarket chain to design, plan, and implement a campaign targeting specific groups of consumers.

Tasks (Before entering a contract with a national supermarket chain):

1. Develop statement of the purpose of the campaign to address the bakery's strategic outcome.
2. Determine the contribution of the campaign to the bakery's financial outcome. The target is to increase sales by 20 percent; the marketing campaign could be set to contribute 15 percent of the 20 percent increase in sales.
3. Develop the budget for the campaign.
4. Identify the marketing capabilities required to achieve the campaign objectives (e.g., data analytics expertise, access to target audience data)
5. Research the capabilities and costs of marketing services offered by national supermarket chains where Mora's Bakery provides products.
6. Create a proposal to contract the marketing services of one of the national supermarket chains.
7. Choose two national supermarket chains and request a proposal from each.
8. Obtain proposals from the selected supermarket chains and compare pricing and services.
9. Review and assess the proposals to determine the best fit for the campaign. Consider factors such as cost, data analytics expertise, and access to target audience data (e.g., purchase history, preferences, behaviors of each customer by zip code, store, etc.).
10. Collaborate with Mora's Bakery's legal counsel to develop a contract with the chosen supermarket chain, clearly outlining deliverables, timelines, and roles for both Mora's Bakery and the supermarket's marketing team.

Tasks (Following the establishment of a contract with a national supermarket chain):

1. Schedule regular meetings with the supermarket's marketing team.
2. Ensure the supermarket's marketing team has a clear understanding of the target audience and the brand values of the products being promoted.
3. Determine the timeline and clearly outline the tasks for the three components of the marketing campaign: digital ad (advertising in digital platforms like social media, search engines, websites, and mobile apps) and targeted email marketing (sending emails to loyalty card members who purchased Mora's products in the past and the store's newsletter subscribers who bought the product or showed an interest), and in-store promotions (posting ads in the stores).
4. Establish a communication plan with the supermarket's marketing team to provide regular updates on campaign progress, challenges, and opportunities.
5. Work with the supermarket's marketing team to determine the factors to consider in segmentation, such as purchase history, preferences, and behaviors of each customer, segmented by zip code and store, etc.
6. Collaborate with the supermarket's marketing team to develop creative content and materials, such as emails, social media posts, display ads, and promotional materials.
7. Review and approve any marketing materials and messaging developed by the supermarket's marketing team to ensure brand consistency and alignment with campaign objectives.
8. Ensure that the supermarket's marketing team implements and utilizes the tracking and analytics tools as outlined in Item 3 to measure campaign performance.
9. Coordinate with the supermarket's marketing team for the deployment of the campaign.
10. Monitor and analyze campaign results with the supermarket's marketing team to refine the marketing strategy over the campaign's duration.
11. Work with the supermarket's marketing team to adjust the marketing strategy as needed based on the results of the campaign.
12. Track the increase in revenue.
13. Conduct a post-campaign evaluation with the supermarket's marketing team to identify areas of success, areas for improvement, and key learnings to apply to future campaigns.

In Figure 6.2, we revisited the barriers that Mora identified in her Envision step that need attention in the Act step. As an example, we will only focus on one of Mora's barriers to success—her operational processes, including the absence of written or incomplete electronic versions for production, sales and marketing, human resources, finance and accounting, IT, customer support, and administration. After listing the tasks needed to develop the documentation for her operational processes, Mora used Project for the web to capture all the tasks in one place.

Figure 6.2 shows Mora's list of tasks, but each task needs an assigned responsible party and due date within Project for the web. The software tool allows Mora to indicate dependencies. For example, Task 1.9 (uploading new processes to the cloud) cannot be completed until 1.1-1.8 are complete.

Fig. 6.2. Example: Activities and Tasks to Overcome Barriers to Growth #1—Operational Processes

Action Plan Section 2: Overcoming the Bakery's Barriers to Growth Year 1
Outcome Category: Digital Transformation
Outcome: Consistency in operations, guarantee quality, and facilitate staff training
Period: Q1
KPI: Completed Standard Operating Procedures (SOPs) and workflows
Strategy: Develop and implement comprehensive SOPs and workflows to overcome barrier #1 (3.1): The lack or incompleteness of operational processes and training protocols, in both written and electronic forms.
Activity: Develop SOPs and workflows
Tasks

1. Develop a clear goal for the SOPs and workflows and outline their benefits.
2. Share the goal and benefits with staff and address any questions or concerns.
3. Review SOP and workflows for each step of the bakery's process (purchasing, mixing, shaping dough, proofing, baking, packaging, and distribution) and categorize their status completed (ready for training staff), incomplete (missing sections), refine (need revisions), and obsolete (discard).
4. Develop SOPs and workflows based on the categorization in Task 3.1.1
5. Develop a checklist to observe the crews doing their tasks.
6. Observe the different crews twice a week for two weeks to observe how they execute their tasks.
7. Adjust SOPs and workflows based on observations.
8. Train one crew on the new SOPs and workflows and observe the execution for a month.
9. Observe the crew using the checklist.
10. Revise the SOPs and workflows based on the crew's feedback and observations.
11. Upload the SOPs and workflows to the cloud.
12. Celebrate the completion of the SOPs and workflows with the staff and discuss next steps.

Activity: Develop Training Material for Production
Tasks

13. Determine if videos are the best option to train the rest of the staff on SOP and workflows. If so, develop videos as a learning aid, not a substitute for written SOPs and workflows.
14. Schedule training of staff
15. Train the rest of the staff using the new videos, SOPs, and workflows.
16. Post the SOPs and workflows in the most appropriate places at the bakery.
17. Schedule reviews of training.

Your task list should be as comprehensive as possible, but don't be discouraged if you miss a step and have to add it later. This is how action plans evolve, and the growth and discovery that is part of the process. Mora must be patient and set realistic deadlines. Again, the keys are patience and thoroughness.

After you load your project management tool with tasks, assigned responsibilities, deadlines, required resources, dependencies, and whatever other feature you need for your project, you will ask yourself: Is the action plan ready to be executed? Be careful before you give yourself a quick "yes." Check, and double check, to avoid big problems down the road. I have seen implementation efforts fail all too often because of poor planning and lack of detail in the action plan. Review the plan with your team to make sure all possibilities and execution details are addressed.

ACT PART 3: EXECUTING THE ACTION PLAN

An action plan is only as effective as its execution. Even with a well-developed plan that outlines specific activities, tasks, and timelines, the key to success lies in the ability to effectively execute it. This is the crucial stage where your plan is put to the test, and your team must be ready to dig in and get the job done.

Figure 6.3 provides a checklist to assist you in executing your plan.

Fig. 6.3. Action Plan Checklist

Items	Completed	Not Completed	If Not Completed, Set a Date for Completion
BEFORE EXECUTION			
ACTION PLAN REVIEW			
• Each activity has a statement of purpose and desired outcome.			
• Each strategy is linked to one of the four SEAM outcomes: financial, customers, partners, and people.			
• Each activity is linked to a strategy.			
• Tasks under each activity are distinct and not combined or conflated.			
• Tasks are prioritized according to dependencies and deadlines.			
• Resources (people, budget, equipment) are allocated for each activity or task.			
• Start and end dates are visible for each task.			
COMMUNICATION AND COLLABORATION TOOL REVIEW			
• Select a tool to facilitate team communication and collaboration.			
• Establish protocol for team communication and collaboration.			
• Establish protocol for addressing challenges in achieving desired outcomes and interpersonal conflicts.			
• Assign a historian to document changes in action plan and manage the communication and collaboration tool.			
• Test the tool with the team.			
MONITOR PROGRESS AGAINST TIMELINE, PURPOSE, AND DESIRED OUTCOMES			
• Determine the schedule for BAR meetings (before an activity or a task starts).			
• Write BAR questions.			

Items	Completed	Not Completed	If Not Completed, Set a Date for Completion
• Determine the schedule for AAR meetings (after an activity or task ends).			
• Write AAR questions.			
DURING EXECUTION			
• Adjust work plan and timeline based on the AAR meetings.			
• Document changes in action plan and rationale for the change..			
• Remind team of the purpose and desired outcomes.			
• Proactively identify and address potential risks and challenges for each activity.			
• Share results, including successes, challenges, and lessons learned.			
POST EXECUTION			
• Assess the degree to which the desired outcomes were achieved.			
• Celebrate the completion of the project.			
• Share results, including successes, challenges, and lessons learned.			

As depicted in Figure 6.1 of Act Part 2, one of Mora's key strategies to reach her financial objectives involves driving sales growth via a meticulously designed marketing campaign. This campaign employs segmentation techniques effectively, considering factors such as consumers' lifestyle, purchasing habits, demographic information, geographical locations, along with the accommodation of individual allergies and dietary restrictions.

Every task and activity within the action plan serves a crucial role in propelling the business towards this anticipated outcome. Mora projects that the supermarket's focused marketing efforts will contribute 15 percent towards achieving the bakery's financial outcome of 20 percent growth in Q3. The success of her strategy depends on this marketing campaign reaching its specific target contribution of 15 percent.

Given the pivotal role of the marketing campaign, it is imperative to select the right national supermarket chain to design, plan, and implement the marketing strategy. The following elaborates on Mora's thought process behind this selection.

Mora considered three out of the five supermarket chains that carry her bread. All three chains have a strong focus on healthy and organic products, and her sales performance in these chains is robust. The other two are capable of handling only smaller orders. This prevents profitable distributions because Mora's drivers must check each store's inventory weekly to replenish fresh bread. Mora incurs financial losses whenever her drivers must remove or discard expired bread found on the shelves.

After a thorough review of proposals from two national supermarket chains, Mora decides to contract with AllFresh, renowned for its extensive purchase data and data analytics expertise. Mora is confident that a targeted marketing campaign with this national supermarket will reach the broadest customer base effectively. Below are the key characteristics that led Mora to select AllFresh:

- ***First-Party data:*** AllFresh directly collects and owns data from its customers, including demographics, purchases, preferences, and behaviors. AllFresh can target new customers with specific characteristics directly online or at the store with enticing offers to buy Lora's bread.

- **Longitudinal data:** Captures customer's buying patterns, preferences, and habits over time. AllFresh's longitudinal data shows the performance of Mora's bread with loyalty customers over the past eight years she has supplied the store. Such longitudinal data will help Mora gain insights into the purchasing behaviors of past customers and enable Mora to target them over time.

- **Machine learning:** Uses AI and computer algorithms to create predictive models. These models can help identify which customers are most likely to respond to a particular promotion, purchase a specific product, or churn (stop using a product or service). AllFresh can use machine learning to analyze key variables (e.g., age and neighborhoods with higher demand for Mora's bread) enabling them to effectively target potential households for Mora's products and accurately identify likely purchasers.

- **Return-on-ad spending:** Data demonstrates the true incremental impact of advertising by matching ad exposures to verified sales. This enables brand owners to assess campaign performance and adjust investments through detailed analytics that track customers who bought the product based on scanned barcodes. Such insights will help Mora make informed decisions regarding her advertising budget.

- **Sales monitoring:** Provides brand owners with insights into their product's in-store and online sales performance, directly resulting from advertising campaigns executed across various AllFresh properties.

- **Data Science Division:** AllFresh's experienced team can determine the true influence of digital media by accounting for purchases that would have occurred even without advertising efforts. With this information, Mora gains a more accurate understanding of her brand's organic sales performance within the store.

Besides following her action plan within her project management tool, Mora uses another excellent tool to organize her thoughts—a logic model. In my experience, there are three things that ensure successful execution of a project—research, a project management tool, and the use of a logic model.

THE LOGIC MODEL FOR THE MARKETING CAMPAIGN

Remember the logic model from Chapter 2? As you outline the tasks for your strategies, the logic model can serve as a valuable tool to help you systematically organize your thoughts around the resources you possess, the necessary activities, the expected outputs, and the desired outcomes. Mora employed this model as a visual aid in planning the marketing campaign, thereby gaining a comprehensive overview of what she aimed to achieve.

She continuously revised the activities, outputs, and outcomes in the model based on her collaborative discussions with AllFresh and according to her budget for the marketing campaign. As depicted in Figure 6.4, these revisions encapsulate the comprehensive understanding developed from her interaction with AllFresh. Many of these meticulously planned activities found their place in her contract with AllFresh and in the final action plan

Mora greatly valued the simplicity of the logic model in illustrating her vision for the marketing campaign. Just as crucially, its systematic layout streamlined the communication of her expectations to AllFresh. We highly recommend using a logic model when creating your own action plans - it can be a game changer in planning and achieving your strategic goals!

Fig. 6.4. Illustration of Supermarket Strategy Using Logic Model

Inputs **Sample Activities** **Sample Inputs** **Sample Outcomes**

- Budget
- Bread
- Brand reputation
- Bakery's staff time
- AllFresh's purchase data
- AllFresh's team of data science
- AllFresh's machine learning algorithms
-

Marketing Campaign:

1. Display digital ads across the web targeting the buyer persona.
2. Custom landing page on AllFresh.com.
3. Targeted digital coupons on AllFresh online channels
4. Product listing ads on AllFresh website
5. Targeted email to shoppers with loyalty card

---

1. Display digital ads across the web targeting the buyer persona
   - *Impressions*: how many times your ads were displayed
   - *Clicks*: how many times your ads were clicked on
   - *Conversions*: how many of those clicks led to the desired action, such as a purchase or sign-up
2. Custom landing page on AllFresh.com
   - *Page Visits*: total number of visits to the page
   - *Bounce Rate*: percentage of visitors who leave after viewing only one page
   - *Conversion Rate*: percentage of visitors who perform the desired action on the page, such as filling out a form or making a purchase
   - *Average Time on Page*: average amount of time visitors spent on the page.
3. Targeted digital coupons on AllFresh online channels
   - *Coupon Downloads/Claims*: total number of coupons downloaded or claimed
   - *Redemption Rate*: how many of the coupons were actually used to make a purchase
   - *Sales from Coupon Redemptions*: total sales resulting from these coupon redemptions
4. Product listing ads on AllFresh website
   - *Impressions*: how often the ads are displayed
   - *Clicks*: how often the ads are clicked on
   - *Conversions*: how often those clicks lead to a purchase
5. Targeted email to shoppers with loyalty card
   - *Open Rate*: the percentage of recipients who open the email
   - *Click-Through Rate*: the percentage of those who clicked on a link within the email
   - *Conversion Rate*: the percentage who made a purchase or completed another desired action
   - *Unsubscribe Rate*: the percentage of recipients who opted out of receiving future emails

---

- Increased Sales
- Increased Revenue
- Higher Return on Investment (ROI)
- Improved Customer Retention and Loyalty
- Market Share Growth
- Brand Awareness and Reputation
- Sales Lift
- Brand Lift

To aid in completing your Act step, all the figures and blank templates are available in appendix 1 at the end of the book.

The Act step is an exciting one as you begin to see how your strategies advance and transform your business or organization. Remember, tweaking the plan as needed is very normal and encouraged. However, you won't know how well your strategies have performed until you enter the last stage of the SEAM framework—Measure.

Chapter 7

SEAM Step 4: MEASURE

"For a successful life, or successful business, measure what you want to improve."

Jerry Bruckner

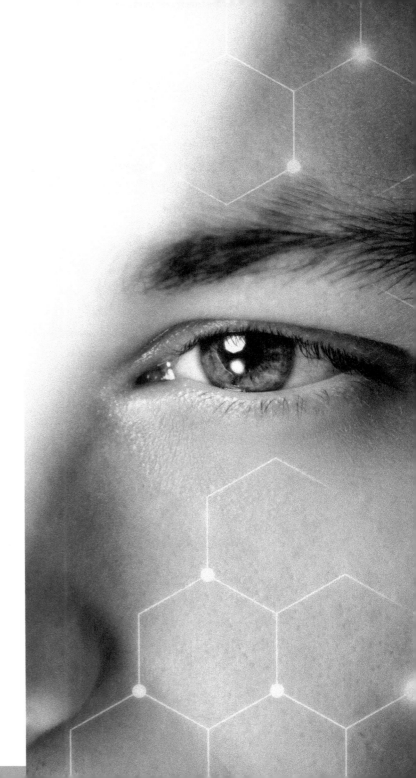

I n my work as a consultant and with the SEAM model, I consider measurement my "daily bread." Just as bread is a staple food we consume daily, measuring progress is a staple activity in Windrose Vision, my consulting company. Regardless of the sector—be it private, public, academic, or non-profit—my clients seek to understand the ROI of their efforts. They also strive to leverage data for informed decision-making and future outcome setting.

WHY MEASURE YOUR TRANSFORMATION JOURNEY?

The "M" in SEAM stands for the Measure step. The focal point of the SEAM Measure step lies in assessing the extent to which you have reached your business outcomes—financial, customer, partner, and people, as well as your digital transformation outcomes outlined in your action plan from the Act step. In the Measure step, we compare the KPIs established in the Envision step with the actual results we achieved from implementing our strategies. Your KPIs should measure your outcomes.

So, what can we expect from our transformation journey?

INSIGHT INTO TRANSFORMATIVE EFFECTS: The Measure step allows you to evaluate the tangible impacts of digital technology on your business operations. These may include enhancements in efficiency, production consistency, or uplifts in customer satisfaction.

Highlighting performance and improvement areas: Through measurement, you can identify the sectors contributing most significantly to business outcomes and those requiring additional adjustments or support to optimize their contribution.

VALIDATING FINANCIAL COMMITMENTS: The Measure step plays a crucial role in validating expenditures by not only demonstrating ROI but also by showcasing how the technology investment translates into improved financial outcomes. This information underpins future decisions regarding resource allocation for optimum business performance.

STRATEGIC PLANNING: Gauging the effects of integrating current technology into your business will help you to formulate your future digital strategy. The insights you glean will enable you to determine how your business can leverage technological trends to reach desired business outcomes. Your business will become more competitive in the ever-evolving digital business landscape.

IDENTIFYING TRAINING NEEDS: Measurement can shed light on your team's adaptability to new technologies—a factor directly influencing productivity and, consequently, business outcomes. It can pinpoint areas where additional training might be essential.

TIPS FOR YOUR MEASURE STEP

Your Measure step will depend on your first three steps of SEAM. However, regardless of the set outcomes in your business or organization, there are a few things you need to know to make your Measure step as effective as possible.

REGULARLY REVIEW AND ADAPT: Consistently assess your KPIs to gauge the efficacy of your strategies toward achieving your outcomes. Modify these measures and strategies in line with shifting priorities, needs, and market conditions.

TRAIN YOUR MANAGEMENT TEAM: Ensure that your management team is on board with the KPIs you measure for success. They should understand and apply the practices of tracking and monitoring progress. Tracking involves recording completed tasks and milestones outlined in your action plan, while monitoring encompasses assessing performance, identifying trends, and taking proactive steps to address deviations or challenges.

TRACK PROGRESS IN REAL TIME: Use a tool to track progress in real time. Tracking provides a comparison of actual progress against the planned milestones. This will give everyone involved in the action plan visibility into what's happening and how much is left to complete.

KEEP DATA ACCESSIBLE: Use dashboards or other visualization tools to present data clearly and understandably. Making data easily accessible will encourage regular tracking and monitoring of performance.

RECOGNIZE AND REWARD PROGRESS: Celebrate achievements and progress based on measured results. Recognize individuals and teams who consistently meet or exceed performance targets. This recognition can motivate staff to strive for their personal best on the job.

Most importantly, be patient.

MORA'S MEASURE STEP

Currently, Mora's Bakery is progressing into Q3 of SEAM Year 2. Throughout SEAM Years 1 and 2, Mora recalibrated her strategies and modified the timelines for specific activities and tasks in her dynamic action plans. This continuous fine-tuning was deemed crucial in the face of the dual challenge of implementing new technologies and systems while continuing to operate within the status quo. As Mora pursued the bakery's business outcomes—financial, customer, partner, and people—she grappled with the complex task of generating a new era of automation and digital integration within her bakery's ecosystem. She had to deploy new equipment, digitize various processes, implement a comprehensive staff training program, and foster an environment conducive to positive work relationships. This multifaceted journey speaks to Mora's resilience and adaptability as she navigates the bakery's transformation journey.

For SEAM Year 1, Mora monitored her progress toward achieving her business outcomes by comparing her anticipated KPI targets with her actual performance. Moving into SEAM Year 2, she used the actual results from the first year as a benchmark to assess, develop, and revise her outcomes for the upcoming year. Consequently, she updated her KPIs to align with the adjusted expectations.

With the close of SEAM Year 2 on the horizon, Mora must begin contemplating her outcomes for SEAM Year 3. As she evaluates her progress in the second year, she will shape her third-year outcomes based on the results of SEAM Year 2.

SEAM STEP 4: MEASURE
PART 1: Outcomes in SEAM Year 1
PART 2: Outcomes in SEAM Year 2
PART 3: Integrated Business and Digital Transformation Outcomes in SEAM Year 3

MEASURE PART 1: OUTCOMES IN SEAM YEAR 1

KEY HIGHLIGHTS

Mora's action plan for Year 1 meticulously outlined the activities, tasks, and timelines associated with each strategy, aiming to reach four categories of business outcomes—financial, customer, partner, and people. She monitored progress by comparing actual quarterly performance against her projected KPI targets. This information then guided her adjustments to the activities and their associated tasks within the action plan.

Mora delineated two process-oriented outcomes to be accomplished by the end of Year One: 1) the effortless installation, setup, and integration of the ERP system, a dough shaper, and packaging equipment into the bakery's operations, and 2) the implementation of comprehensive training programs for the bakery staff, ensuring their proficiency in using the new tools. She monitored progress toward these process-oriented outcomes by comparing the projected due dates in the action plan with the actual completion dates. Tracking was done in real-time so team members could receive immediate feedback on their progress. Mora demonstrated excellent oversight of performance. She anticipated potential risks, such as delays in equipment installation, and adjusted the plan proactively to ensure minimal disruption.

Figure 7.1 shows the highlights of Mora's action plan in SEAM Year 1, broken down by quarters. In Q1, Mora incorporated the outcomes, strategies, and KPIs from the bakery's annual business plan that she had developed into the SEAM framework. After completing the first two steps of SEAM (Snapshot and Envision), she focused on developing an action plan to implement the revised strategies, along with the new ones, for the recently defined outcomes.

In Q2, Mora began implementing her action plan. This included delving into the research for purchasing a new ERP system and the best new equipment vendor for the bakery equipment. She also explored the marketing services at the national supermarkets that sold her bread and decided that AllFresh was her best option.

Mora contracted AllFresh and began working closely with them to implement the marketing campaign in Q3. The targeted marketing campaign launched and ended in Q3. Meanwhile, she selected the ERP vendor and started preparing for installation.

In Q4, Mora finished implementing the ERP system. Also, as is always the case at the year-end, it was time for Mora to start looking at her SEAM action plan for Year 2.

Fig. 7.1 Key Highlights from Year 1 Action Plan Execution

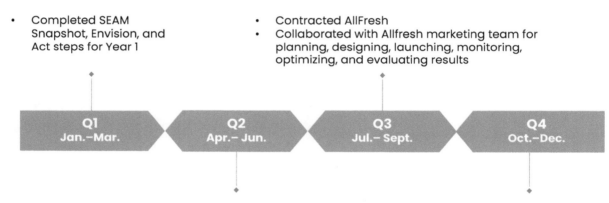

- Completed SEAM Snapshot, Envision, and Act steps for Year 1

- Contracted AllFresh
- Collaborated with Allfresh marketing team for planning, designing, launching, monitoring, optimizing, and evaluating results

Q1 Jan.–Mar.   **Q2** Apr.– Jun.   **Q3** Jul.– Sept.   **Q4** Oct.–Dec.

- Started implementing SEAM Action Plan
- Researched different ERP systems, examined various bakery equipment options, tested the most promising choices, and met with several vendors to make the best decision for the bakery

- Implemented ERP system
- Started developing SEAM Action Plan for Year 2

FINANCIAL OUTCOMES

Mora compared her projected financial outcome to the actual performance of the bakery and the result was amazing! Mora not only achieved her revenue target of $2,035,277.50 but exceeded it by 25 percent, reaching a remarkable total of $2,544,096.875! Most of her revenue growth was in Q3 and Q4.

STRATEGY FOR SUPERMARKETS: By meticulously outlining the activities and tasks for each strategy, Lora was able to stay on track, resulting in an increase in sales. This was especially true for her strategy to launch a targeted marketing campaign with one of her supermarket customers, AllFresh.

AllFresh was stunned by the results of the digital ad campaign, which targeted Mora's buyer persona. AllFresh conducted customer segmentation for Mora's prospective patrons, taking into account aspects like lifestyle, purchasing behaviors, demographic profiles, and nutritional preferences, including non-dairy, nut-free, and vegan options, as well as geographical locations (based on store location) among other criteria. Mora saw a 30 percent increase in sales and a 10 percent lift (additional sales generated during the campaign compared to deals that would have occurred without any marketing activity). As shown in Figure 7.2, Mora's buyer persona considers a broader age range, acknowledging that health-conscious consumers are found across different generations. All of the individuals in her target market share common traits like a preference for health-oriented, quality products, a willingness to pay for them, and a lifestyle that aligns with the values represented by Mora's brand.

Fig. 7.2 Mora's Buyer Persona

Mora's Buyer Persona: The Health-Conscious Bread Lover

✓ *Demographics*: The target demographic extends beyond millennial and Generation Z consumers. It also includes health-conscious older adults and seniors who possess the purchasing power to afford artisanal bread. These individuals place a high value on quality and are willing to pay a premium for it.

✓ *Geographics*: Mora's customers reside in the same zip codes as AllFresh store locations, potentially indicating urban or suburban areas where artisanal bread is more readily available.

✓ *Behaviors*: Individuals in this persona includes not only regular customers but also potential customers who prioritize quality and health in their food choices. They are willing to invest in superior, artisanal products like Mora's bread.

✓ *Lifestyle* and interests: These customers lead a health-conscious lifestyle and highly value nutrition. They show interest in non-dairy and nut-free options, possibly due to dietary restrictions, health reasons, or a preference for variety. These individuals are likely well-educated about food and health.

✓ *Needs and challenges*: Individuals in this persona seek high-quality, nutritious bread that fits within their health-focused lifestyle. They appreciate transparency about ingredients and nutritional content. They may face challenges in finding such specialized products that meet their quality standards and dietary needs.

✓ *Motivations*: These individuals are motivated by maintaining a healthy lifestyle and the desire for high-quality, tasty food. They are drawn to brands that align with their values and offer products that cater to their dietary needs and preferences.

The marketing campaign consisted of 1) digital ads in social media, search engines, websites, and mobile apps; 2) targeted emails to both loyalty card members who purchased Mora's products in the past and the store's newsletter's subscribers who bought the product or showed an interest; and 3) in-store promotions consisting of ads posted in the stores. AllFresh campaign results confirmed Mora's findings about millennials and Generation Z liking and purchasing her artisanal bread.

AllFresh analyzed customer exposure, participation, and sales to understand what worked throughout the campaign. The weekly reporting tools evaluated the ROAS (results on advertising spend) and showed that the ROAS improved as the campaign progressed. The campaigns ran against specific AllFresh audiences to compare which segments drove the most volume. Mora could then efficiently place more of her ad spend against those targets.

Because of her success with specific audiences, Mora and the AllFresh team decided she should offer the bread in more stores with extensive home delivery within selected zip codes where health-conscious bread lovers reside. More frequent deliveries would help Mora reduce the amount of bread likely to expire on supermarket shelves.

STRATEGY FOR RESTAURANTS: In her Act step, Mora developed a strategy to promote the health benefits and environmental impact of vegan, non-dairy, and nut-free bread products. She hoped that this strategy would boost her sales to new restaurants set to open near the new corporate headquarters in town. However, when the new company opened, she lost a couple of her larger restaurant customers, but gained some medium-sized restaurants that offered healthy choice menus and targeted vegan and vegetarian diners. Mora attributes her success in recruiting new restaurants to following her plan and offering tailored menu suggestions and recipes to the new restaurants.

CUSTOMER OUTCOMES

Mora established the outcome of cultivating a customer-centric culture, with her initial first year focused exclusively on restaurants. She wanted to collect helpful insights from restaurant patrons to comprehend their needs and preferences, with the intent of using the feedback to address those concerns. However, she could not find a foolproof way to measure the satisfaction of restaurant owners, chefs, or managers with her products. First, Mora emailed a five-question, multiple-choice online survey to the restaurants' managers, but nobody responded. Next, she tried to schedule time with the restaurant owners to gather their input but was unsuccessful because they thought it was just an opening to sell them more bread. She then asked the delivery drivers to solicit feedback from people who received her products at the restaurants. Drivers often forgot to ask or did not remember who gave them the feedback. The data that was collected was unreliable.

Mora's experience shows us that our strategies often go differently than planned. Some strategies go better than expected (the digital marketing campaign), while others aren't as effective (the efforts to gather customer feedback). Sometimes we gain surprise benefits from our efforts. For example, the digital marketing campaign with AllFresh had the happy consequence of developing a stronger relationship with the chain. Mora can now consider AllFresh her customer as well as her partner.

This means her definition of partner will be revised when she develops her outcomes for Year 3.

PARTNER OUTCOMES

Mora made progress toward her partner outcome of nurturing her strategic partnerships. You may recall that Mora wanted to strengthen existing partnerships and build new ones by formalizing verbal agreements and articulating the purpose of the partnerships. Mora successfully signed memorandums of understanding (MOUs) with each of the two artisanal bakeries she had successfully worked with. One of the relationships paid off in another way by providing a valuable referral to the SAP ERP consultant.

While examining various ERP systems and bakery machines, she had the opportunity to converse with multiple bakeries and began establishing connections with them. However, she found herself extremely busy due to the demands of managing her bakery during its initial year, which involved purchasing equipment, training staff, and other tasks. Nonetheless, she recognized the importance of nurturing these new relationships for future endeavors.

PEOPLE OUTCOMES

Mora made reasonable progress on her outcome to foster ownership of the work among her team. You may remember she had two specific strategies to achieve these outcomes.

INSTITUTE A PEER-TO-PEER RECRUITMENT INITIATIVE: Her idea to offer incentives to the staff if the bakery was successful in meeting its desired financial outcome. The staff was happy with the bonuses, and many of them referred other potential staff members to the bakery, hoping to receive a bonus. (The referral had to remain employed for six months for the referring staff member to collect.) Mora felt the incentives increased morale, as did the digital marketing campaign. The staff was excited to see Mora's Bakery products featured in the supermarket campaign online and in stores. They were proud to have made the bread from Mora's Bakery, and some team members were even featured in the promotional ads, on the internet, and in the local stores.

APPLY ELEMENTS OF AGILE METHODOLOGY (SELF-ORGANIZING TEAMS): Mora encountered several challenges as she implemented flexible work shifts, role rotation, and peer-to-peer learning. For example, the bakery team sometimes overstaffed or understaffed the bakery, took longer to complete tasks as they navigated unfamiliar roles (e.g., mixing to packaging bread), and needed help making decisions. Mora sent her manager to train on the self-organizing model since traditionally blue-collar jobs have clear, predefined roles and responsibilities, and a shift to a self-organizing model requires workers to adapt to a broader range of tasks, learn new skills quickly and efficiently, and develop new soft skills like communication, collaboration, and conflict resolution. To mitigate these difficulties, Mora offered consistent support and reassurances to her team as her manager provided training and scheduling and created open lines of communication for feedback and queries.

Mora understood that introducing automation and digital technologies into her bakery's processes could cause job insecurity among her bakery team. Figure 7.3 describes Mora's strategies to navigate the transition smoothly while maintaining team morale and productivity.

Fig. 7.3. Mora's Strategies for Maintaining Morale and Productivity

✓ *Transparent communication*: Mora prioritized transparency about the forthcoming changes, explaining the reasons for automation, its impact on the business, and expected changes for the bakery's team.

✓ *Reassure team members*: She reassured her bakery's team that automation might decrease their hours but wouldn't necessarily result in job loss; instead, it would enhance efficiency and enable team members to undertake more value-added activities.

✓ *Upskill and reskill team members*: Mora offered training for her bakery's team to work with the new technology. Reskilling enabled them to adapt to new roles required of automation. Upskilling helped them enhance their existing competencies.

✓ *Role evolution, not replacement*: She emphasized that automation would take over repetitive tasks, allowing team members to focus on more creative, customer-centric, or strategic aspects of the business, viewing automation as a work enhancer rather than a threat.

✓ *Involve team members in the process*: Mora engaged her bakery's team in the automation process from the selection to the implementation stages. Their input made the system more effective, and their involvement reduced resistance to change by fostering a sense of ownership.

✓ *Career development opportunities*: She highlighted how automation could open new opportunities for career growth within the bakery, including roles in customer service, product development, or tech support for the new automated processes.

DIGITAL TRANSFORMATION OUTCOMES IN YEAR 1

In Year 1, Mora prioritized developing SOPs and workflows to ensure operational consistency, quality assurance, and efficient staff training. This priority directly addressed Barrier #1 in Operational Processes: The absence of comprehensive, documented operational processes and training protocols, whether in written or electronic form. Mora did an excellent job outlining all the tasks for the SOPs in the action plan, so her management team followed them, and they could finish according to the schedule. In SEAM Year 1, Mora completed all her SOPs and workflows in an electronic form. She also created new training videos to retrain her staff and introduce the new SOPs and workflows.

Mora then turned her attention to the second barrier—her need for ERP. During her Envision step, Mora had considered streamlining the bakery's processes with ERP software and recognized the significant advantage of integrating the packaging machine and dough shaping equipment with the ERP system. This integration would allow seamless communication and data exchange between the machinery and the ERP system, enabling real-time monitoring, inventory management, and automated data capture.

However, the undertaking of engaging with vendors and securing the dough shaping and packaging machines introduced greater complexity and time demands than originally estimated. Mora found herself in deep strategic thought, projecting the future needs of the bakery in terms of equipment. By Q3 of Year 1, it became apparent that the timeline needed adjustment. The installation of the dough shaping and packaging machines would now be accomplished by Q2 of Year 2, followed by a dedicated period for staff training in Q3.

Mora made a strategic decision to leverage the accounting capabilities of the ERP system, as opposed to fixating on the equipment installation delays. The bakery's financial information is scattered across multiple Excel spreadsheets, making consolidation and analysis difficult. With the integration of accounting functionalities within the ERP system, Mora could unify her financial data, automate processes, and gain comprehensive insights through dashboards and reports. This could facilitate her in tracking financial outcomes, monitoring KPIs, and making informed decisions based on data.

As recommended, Mora involved key team members and consulted industry experts to ensure she considered everything. She looked for four factors in her selection of an ERP system:

- *Business needs alignment:* The right ERP system should cater to the bakery's unique needs, industry specifics, and potential future growth.
- *Usability and flexibility:* The ERP system should be intuitive, easy to use, customizable, and adaptable to the bakery's unique processes.
- *Integration capabilities:* The ERP system should seamlessly integrate with existing or future software, hardware, and equipment for smooth data exchange and workflow.
- *Reliable vendor:* The vendor should have a solid reputation, providing dependable support and regular updates. They also should offer comprehensive training and have a history of long-term commitment to customers, specifically small businesses. In addition, the vendor should have a reputation for working collaboratively with other bakery equipment

suppliers (e.g., the manufacturer or vendor of the dough shaper).

Meanwhile, she also was working on a partner outcome—to formalize her relationships with other smaller artisanal bakeries who could assist her with capacity. In speaking with the owner of one of them, she obtained the name of a consultant who specialized in SAP ERP. SAP stands for Systems, Applications, and Products in Data Processing, a software company based in Germany that provides ERP software to businesses and organizations of all types and sizes. The SAP ERP business management software offers many modules of interest to Mora's Bakery, including production planning (which would support the traceability of ingredients used in Mora's finished products), financial accounting, process management, quality management, and more. Mora found herself particularly excited about the financial accounting module and the ability to add more modules as she grew. She arranged a meeting with the referred SAP vendor and several others, applied the criteria listed above, and signed a contract with the SAP ERP that she felt best fit her needs.

MEASURE PART 2: OUTCOMES IN SEAM YEAR 2

In SEAM Year 2, Mora also divided her action plan into two sections: business outcomes and digital transformation outcomes. She formulated business outcomes for Year 2 using SEAM Year 1's performance as a foundational benchmark.

FINANCIAL OUTCOME

Mora opted to raise her revenue forecast with the rise in her revenue during SEAM Year 1. Subsequently, she tweaked the KPI targets for sales to correspond with this change. This adjustment involved a steady quarterly increase of 10 percent from the previous year's figures, peaking with a 15 percent jump in Q4. To reach these KPIs, she retained her two strategies from Year 1. For the supermarkets, she envisioned a scaled-down version of the AllFresh marketing campaign. At the same time, she planned to promote the benefits of serving healthy bread to the restaurants. Her two strategies were successful, and she met her KPI sales targets as of Q3.

CUSTOMER OUTCOME

Mora retained her SEAM Year 1 and Year 2 outcomes to create a customer-centric culture. This is an ongoing outcome that requires a shift in strategy. Since she could not gather input through surveys from her restaurant customers, she initiated a quarterly bread-tasting event at one of the AllFresh local stores. The event was beneficial for both Mora's Bakery and AllFresh. At these events, attendees were asked to complete a five-question survey on their phones. As an incentive to encourage participation, Mora offered a free delivery of bread of their choice, selected through a raffle among those who completed the survey. This strategy proved successful, and she received feedback that suggested making the bread loaves smaller. This suggestion aligned well with her research in Year 1 about millennials and Generation Z liking the smaller size of her bread.

PARTNER OUTCOME

Mora's partner outcome for SEAM Year 1 was to cultivate strategic partnerships. However, in the second year, she broadened her understanding of a "partner" to include the

AllFresh supermarket chain. This decision stemmed from the mutually beneficial relationship between AllFresh and her bakery. AllFresh exhibited interest in her artisanal bread, which catered to its customer base, and they were enthusiastic about adding more small businesses to the AllFresh supplier network. Their collaboration thrived, particularly during the design, planning, execution, and post-evaluation stages of the marketing campaign and the development of her buyer persona.

PEOPLE OUTCOME

Mora chose to retain the same outcome for SEAM Year 1 and 2—to foster a sense of ownership among the staff. This morphed into a continuous outcome because of its level of difficulty. Mora found it challenging to implement and maintain self-organizing teams because it required educating her staff about Agile methodology, which was hard to do. She also had to continue reinforcing the concept whenever new staff came aboard. Mora tried her best to keep up with the development of her managers and sustain the widely appreciated peer-to-peer recruitment initiative.

DIGITAL TRANSFORMATION OUTCOMES IN YEAR 2

Mora learned the importance of tracking and monitoring progress in SEAM Year 1. As she implemented major activities in SEAM Year 2, she meticulously tracked her team's tasks against the action plan's timeline. This gave her a snapshot of the advancements toward her business and digital transformation outcomes. However, Mora knew that monitoring progress went beyond tracking completion. It involved continuously evaluating performance (like having the BAR and AAR meeting), identifying risks (like delays in installation of equipment), and taking proactive actions (having staff trained in the use of equipment so they would be ready when the machines were installed).

Figure 7.4 illustrates the significant activities undertaken by Lora in Year 2. With enthusiasm, Lora welcomed the introduction of a new dough machine that ensured uniformity in dough sizes and weights, thereby reducing potential overproduction or waste due to inconsistent portioning. She eagerly anticipated full-time use of the packaging machine, viewing it as a revolutionary addition to the bakery. This machine would alleviate the staff from the monotony of packaging bread manually and eliminate mishaps related to packaging. Lora's staff received comprehensive training on these machines by mid Q4, with the equipment manufacturer's full cooperation.

Integration of both the packaging machine and the dough shaping equipment with the ERP system is set to streamline operations, enhance efficiency, and yield valuable insights for decision-making. This integration represents a significant stride for the bakery.

Fig. 7.4. Key Highlights from Year 2 Action Plan Execution

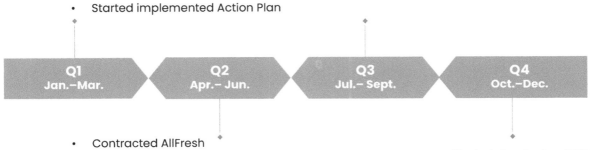

- Completed SEAM Action Plan for Year 2
- Started implemented Action Plan
- Installed shaping dough and packaging equipment
- Trained staff on how to use new equipment

| Q1 Jan.–Mar. | Q2 Apr.– Jun. | Q3 Jul.– Sept. | Q4 Oct.–Dec. |

- Contracted AllFresh
- Collaborated with Allfresh marketing team for planning, designing, launching, monitoring, optimizing, and evaluating results
- Started developing SEAM Action Plan for Year 3

MEASURE PART 3: INTEGRATED BUSINESS AND DIGITAL TRANSFORMATION OUTCOMES IN YEAR 3

Mora started her planning and KPI measurement for the upcoming year from a different point than SEAM Year 1. In SEAM Year 3, Mora can appreciate the intricate weave of automation into tasks like dough shaping and packaging various types of bread. Her ERP system, digitally connected with these machines, illustrates a seamless fusion of business management and advanced automation, improving her grasp of technology's role in modernizing bakery operations.

Now, she can use her ERP system to assist in the tracking and monitoring a wide range of KPIs. Her new baseline for measuring progress will be the bakery operations in Year 3, considering the advancements made in the digitized environment.

FINANCIAL AND CUSTOMER OUTCOMES

Figure 7. 5 shows an assortment of KPI labels that Mora can use to measure progress toward the bakery's two categories of outcomes: financial and customer. It's important to remember that these KPIs are mere illustrations. Mora needs to provide the actual quantifiable measures such as precise numbers, percentages, or other relevant units.

The bakery can increase its profitability by effectively managing costs and achieving a favorable ROI. KPIs such as consistency in production, order accuracy, and customer feedback/ratings directly contribute to customer satisfaction by ensuring that the bakery consistently meets quality standards, accurately fulfills orders, and receives positive customer feedback. Notice that Figure 7.5 includes "improve operational efficiency" as a customer outcome. KPIs like order fulfillment and time and resource utilization play a role in achieving operational efficiency and indirectly impact customer satisfaction. By improving operational efficiency, the bakery can enhance its ability to deliver products promptly, minimize errors, and meet customer expectations regarding service and delivery.

Fig. 7.5. Mora's Bakery Financial and Customer Outcomes and KPIs for Year 3

Category	SEAM Outcome	KPI Label	Description
Financial	Increase Profitability	Return on Investment (ROI)	Net profit of digital transformation investments divided by their cost
	Cost Savings	Cost Savings	Dollar amount saved due to reduced labor, waste, and inefficiencies
	Increase sales	Sales growth	Percentage growth in sales compared to a prior period.
Customer	Enhance Product Quality and Consistency	Consistency in Production	Percentage of products meeting quality standards
		Order Accuracy	Percentage of orders correctly fulfilled
		Customer Feedback/Ratings	Average customer rating (e.g., out of 5 stars)
	Improve Operational Efficiency	Production Time	Number of minutes/hours to produce a batch of goods
		Order Fulfillment Time	Number of minutes/hours from order receipt to readiness for delivery or pick-up
		Resource Utilization	Percentage of ingredients used vs. wasted
		Waste Reduction	Percentage reduction in wasted ingredients
		Inventory Turnover	Number of times inventory is sold or used in a period (e.g., weekly, monthly, quarterly)

You may be wondering about the origin of the KPIs in Figure 7.5 Mora obtained these KPIs from the cost-benefit analysis she conducted as part of the Envision step to assess the potential benefits of purchasing new equipment.

Figure 7.6 visually represents the connection between the bakery's business outcomes and the digital transformation initiatives. The KPIs measure efficiency, productivity, and effectiveness within two of the bakery's specific production processes: shaping dough and packaging.

The ERP system is a vital link between the dough shaper, the packaging machine, and other systems within Mora's bakery. It facilitates seamless communication and data exchange, ensuring accurate instructions and parameters are transmitted to the machines in real time. By leveraging the ERP system's connectivity, Mora can optimize the performance of the dough shaper and the packaging machine, improving operational efficiency, product consistency, and overall bakery productivity.

By considering these KPIs in Figure 7.6 for efficiency, productivity, and effectiveness, Mora can comprehensively understand the bakery's performance in these crucial areas. This information can guide her decision-making process and help her identify areas for improvement as she navigates the digital transformation of her bakery.

- Monitoring efficiency KPIs allows Mora to identify areas where operational streamlining is needed.
- Monitoring productivity KPIs allows Mora to monitor efficient resource allocation and minimize order fulfillment delays.
- Monitoring KPIs to measure effectiveness helps Mora achieve consistent production, maintain a high-quality product, and track order accuracy for increasing customer satisfaction and loyalty.

Fig. 7.6. Connection Between SEAM Business Outcomes and Digital Transformation Outcomes

Category	SEAM Outcomes	KPI Labels	ERP System	Dough Shaper	Packaging Machine	Initial Digital Transformation Outcomes		
						Efficiency	Productivity	Effectiveness
Financial	Increase Profitability	Return on Investment (ROI)	✓	✓	✓			✓
		Cost Savings	✓	✓	✓		✓	
		Sales growth				✓	✓	✓
Customer	Enhance Product Quality and Consistency	Consistency in Production		✓	✓		✓	✓
		Order Accuracy	✓		✓			✓
		Customer Feedback/Ratings	✓	✓	✓			✓
	Improve Operational Efficiency	Production Time	✓	✓	✓	✓	✓	
		Order Fulfillment Time	✓			✓	✓	
		Resource Utilization	✓	✓	✓	✓		
		Waste Reduction	✓	✓				
		Inventory Turnover	✓				✓	

PARTNER OUTCOMES

Figure 7.7 shows two partner outcomes for Mora's Bakery: 1) Establish collaborative partnerships and marketing campaigns with supermarket chains, and 2) Explore partnership opportunities with other bakery companies.

Establish Collaborative Partnerships and Marketing Campaigns with Supermarket Chains: Mora wants to create successful partnerships with other grocery stores like she has with AllFresh. She wants to implement more strategic digital marketing efforts to leverage their customer base and increase the visibility of her brand to drive sales and expand her customer reach. New partnerships will empower Mora to gather even more valuable data and insight and fine-tune her data-driven decision-making.

Explore Partnership Opportunities with Other Bakery Companies: Introducing new digital equipment presents opportunities for partnerships and collaborations beyond supermarket chains. Mora can explore possibilities, such as renting out the use of the equipment to other bakers when it is not in use or becoming a co-packer for another company. With such partnerships, Mora can maximize the value of her equipment, generate additional revenue streams, and foster relationships within the baking industry.

Mora anticipates a spillover effect from her marketing campaign with restaurants. She expects restaurant owners and chefs to seek her out after hearing about her bread products in the advertisements. However, she still needs to formulate her specific objectives for the third year concerning her engagement with restaurants.

Fig. 7.7. Partner Outcomes for Year 3

Category	SEAM Outcome	KPI Label	Purpose
Partner	Establish Collaborative Partnerships and Marketing Campaigns with Supermarket Chains	Number of Partnerships Formed	Measures the number of new partnerships with supermarket chains
		Revenue Generated from Partnerships	Assesses the financial success of the partnerships in terms of sales derived from the supermarkets
		Customer Reach	Quantifies the increase in customers that Mora's bakery products are reaching through supermarket chains
		Brand Visibility	Evaluates changes in awareness and recognition of Mora's brand among consumers due to the partnerships
		Data Gathering and Utilization	Tracks the quantity and quality of consumer data gathered through the partnerships for informed business decisions
	Explore Partnership Opportunities with Other Bakers and Companies	Number of Partnerships Formed	Monitors the number of partnerships with other bakers and companies
		Utilization Rate of Digital Equipment	Evaluates how often Mora's digital baking equipment is being used by other bakers or companies
		Utilization Rate of Digital Equipment	Evaluates how often other bakers or companies are using Mora's digital baking equipment
		Revenue from Partnerships	Measures the additional income generated from partnerships with other bakers and companies
		Innovation and Knowledge Exchange	Assesses new techniques, recipes, or innovations developed through these partnerships

PEOPLE OUTCOMES

As shown in Figure 7.8, Mora's SEAM Year 3 outcome is to "foster a high-performing and empowered bakery team." She wants to continue adapting the self-organizing principles to the bakery in a way that her bakery team can understand and collaborate effectively. She and her team learned a lot, and Mora wants to continue creating a positive work environment that fosters innovation, collaboration, and personal development among the bakery team.

Fig. 7.8. People Outcomes

Category	SEAM Outcome	KPI Label	Purpose
People	Foster a High-Performing and Empowered Bakery Team	Team Productivity	Monitors the team's productivity rates by comparing their output against set targets
		Staff Empowerment Index	Measures the level of staff perception of their empowerment and decision-making authority
		Professional Development	Tracks the progress of staff in terms of training programs attended, new skills acquired, and certifications earned.
		Adaptability Score	Assesses the team's ability to adjust to changes, using feedback forms or performance reviews.
		Employee Satisfaction	Measures the overall job satisfaction, work-life balance, and the effectiveness of recognition initiatives.

THIS IS JUST THE BEGINNING

By adopting the SEAM framework for digital transformation, you'll realize that this journey has a clear starting point but no definitive end. Why? Because technological evolution is boundless, continuously propelling an unending cycle of adaptation and refinement within your business or organization.

For some people, like my father, finding a way to transform their operation could mean the difference between survival and demise. If you never start your digital transformation journey and stop operating long enough to take that Snapshot and think through available technology and what it could mean to your business or organization, the future may pass you by. For business owners like Mora, incorporating both digital and traditional technologies into every aspect of their operations—from decision-making to customer interaction—opens up a world of infinite possibilities. Thanks to the SEAM framework, Mora is now prepared to consider novel value propositions and innovative business models to stay competitive and grow Mora's Bakery even further!

Mora's SEAM framework had a beginning, but the end is nowhere in sight. She will continue to develop and expand her outcomes and KPIs as she reevaluates the bakery's potential with each passing year. She will continue setting relevant KPIs and examining the bakery for barriers keeping her from growth as she marches toward progress, action plan in hand!

SEAM is infinitely rejuvenating. Mora may return to the first step of the SEAM framework and take a new Snapshot of the bakery if she feels the need to Envision a new direction. When she gets to the Measure step, she only needs to review the KPIs from her previous year to see how far she's come.

Mora was grateful for the SEAM framework and its role in creating a new and improved Mora's Bakery. She learned how to set realistic outcomes and KPIs and identify barriers that keep her from growing. Using Project for the web is now second nature to her and her management team as a tool to formulate and monitor action plans. SEAM helped make Mora's Bakery more successful; but on a personal level, it also opened Mora's eyes to new horizons at a time when she thought she had reached her pinnacle.

Now, it's your turn. Is your business or organization ready for the future? To aid you in this journey, all the figures and blank templates are available in appendix 1 at the end of the book.

Also, a quick scan of the accompanying QR code will navigate you directly to my book's website.

I hope that as you are equipped with these tools, you feel prepared and invigorated to put the SEAM framework into action within your business or organization. How will SEAM help your organization thrive? Only you hold the answers to these questions, but one thing remains certain—SEAM can help you prepare for a continually evolving future with everything you need to stay in step with the technology of today and tomorrow.

REFERENCES

Ali, H. 2022. Top 10 Predictions for Baked Goods Trends in 2022. Retrieved from linkedin.com: (February 14) https://www.linkedin.com/pulse/top-10-predictions-baked-goods-trends-2022-hamed-ali/

bcorporation.net. n.d. Measuring a company's Entire Social and Environmental Impact. Retrieved from bcorporation.net: https://www.bcorporation.net/en-us/certification

Berman, K., Knight, J., & Case, J. 2018. Financial Intelligence for Entrepreneurs: What You Really Need to Know About the Numbers. Harvard Business Review Press.

Boardman, A. E., Greenberg, D. H., Vining, A. R., & Weimer, D. L. 2017. Cost-benefit Analysis: Concepts and Practice. Cambridge University Press.

Brousselle, A., & Champagne, F. 2011. Program Theory Evaluation: Logic Analysis. Evaluation and Program Planning, 34(1), 69-78.

Buttle, F. 2009. Customer Relationship Management: Concepts and Technologies (2nd ed.). Routledge.

Connell, J. P., & Kubisch, A. C. 1998. "Applying a Theory of Change Approach to the Evaluation of Comprehensive Community Initiatives: Progress, Prospects, and Problems." New Approaches to Evaluating Community Initiatives, 2(15-44).

Cresanti, R. 2019. "What Small Businesses Know About Corporate Responsibility." October 22. Harvard Business Review.

Cross, R., Gardner, H. K., & Crocker, A. 2021. For an Agile Transformation, Choose the Right People. March-April. Retrieved from hbr.org: https://hbr.org/2021/03/for-an-agile-transformation-choose-the-right-people

Darling, M; Parry, C., & Moore, J. 2005. "Learning in the Thick of it." Harvard Business Review.

Denning, Stephen. 2018. The Age of Agile: How Smart Companies Are Transforming the Way Work Gets Done. HarperCollins Leadership.

Gothelf, Jeff, and Josh Seiden. 2017. Sense and Respond: How Successful Organizations Listen to Customers and Create New Products Continuously. Harvard Business Review Press.

Haddon, H. 2022. "Burger King's New U. S. CEO Seeks to Restore Chain's Luster: Revamp to Direct $400 Million to Advertising and Restaurant Remodels—and the Right Way to Put Cheese on Burgers." October 9. Wall Street Journal.

Juhl, K. 2019. "ABA Unveils Most In-Depth Study on Gen Z Consumers Habits; Reveals Millennial Perceptions of Baked Goods." April 18. Retrieved from americanbakers.org: https://americanbakers. org/news/aba-unveils-most-depth-study-gen-z-consumers-habits-reveals-millennial-perceptions-baked-goods

Knowlton, L. W., & Phillips, C. C. 2013. The Logic Model Guidebook: Better Strategies for Great Results. SAGE Publications.

Kolb, D. A., & Rubin, I. M. 1984. Work as Done vs. Work as Planned: Toward a Different Understanding of Work and Organizations. Journal of Applied Behavioral Science, 20(2), 189-212.

Kotler, P., & Keller, K. L. 2016. Marketing Management (15th ed.). Pearson Education.

Kumar, V., Dixit, A., Javalgi, R. G., & Dass, M. 2021. "Research Framework, Strategies, and Applications of Intelligent Agent Technologies (IATs) in Marketing." Journal of Business Research, 123, 25-45.

Lai, L. 2018. Being a Strategic Leader is About Asking the Right Questions. January 18. Retrieved from Harvard Business Review. https://hbr.org/2017/01/being-a-strategic-leader-is-about-asking-the-right-questions

Larson, E. W., & Gray, C. F. 2021. Project Management: The Managerial Process (8th ed.). McGraw-Hill Education.

Meadows D. H. 2008. Thinking in Systems: A Primer. White River Junction, Vermont: Chelsea Green Publishing.

Mertens, Donna M., & Wilson, Amy T. 2018. Program Evaluation Theory and Practice: A Comprehensive Guide. The Guilford Press.

Mankins, Michael & Gottfredson, Mark. 2022. "Strategy-Making in Turbulent Times: A Dynamic New Model." Harvard Business Review (September–October 2022).

Parmenter, David. 2019. Key Performance Indicators: Developing, Implementing, and Using Winning KPIs. John Wiley & Sons, Inc.

Payne, A., Frow, P., & Eggert, A. 2017. "The Customer Value Proposition: Evolution, Development, and Application in Marketing." Journal of the Academy of Marketing Science, 45(4), 467-489

Rogers, D. L. 2016. The Digital Transformation Playbook: Rethink Your Business for the Digital Age. Columbia Business School Publishing.

Schwaber, K., & Sutherland, J. 2020. The Scrum Guide: The Definitive Guide to Scrum: The Rules of the Game. https://scrumguides.org/docs/scrumguide/v2020/2020-Scrum-Guide-US.pdf

Sharp, S. 2021. Logic Models vs. Theories of Change. March 15. Center for Research Evaluation, University of Mississippi. Retrieved from the blog: https://cere.olemiss.edu/logic-models-vs-theories-of-change/

Siebel, T. M. 2019. Digital Transformation: Surviving and Thriving in an Era of Mass Extinction. RosettaBooks.

Smith, Jane. 2020. Implementing Traceability Systems in the Bakery Industry: Challenges and Opportunities. Baking Business. BakingBusiness.com, Milling & Baking News and Baking & Snacks. (October 2020) https://www.bakingbusiness.com/articles/50807-implementing-traceability-systems-in-the-bakery-industry

Teixeira, Thales S. 2017. "The Power of Anecdotes in Marketing." Harvard Business Review, vol. 95, no. 3, pp. 136-141.

U.S. Copyright Office. 2021. Copyright Law of the United States and Related Laws Contained in Title 17 of the United States Code. Retrieved from https://www.copyright.gov/title17/

U.S. Patent & Trademark Office. 2023. Patent Basics. Retrieved from https://www.uspto.gov/patents/basics.

Weiss, C. H. 1995. Nothing as Practical as Good Theory: Exploring Theory-based Evaluation for Comprehensive Community Initiatives for Children and Families. In J. P. Connell, A. C. Kubisch, L. B. Schorr, & C. H. Weiss (Eds.).

Westerman, G., Bonnet, D., & McAfee, A. 2014. Leading Digital: Turning Technology into Business Transformation. Harvard Business Review Press.

Zeithaml, V. A., Bitner, M. J., & Gremler, D. D. 2017. Services Marketing: Integrating Customer Focus Across the Firm (7th ed.). McGraw-Hill Education.

ABOUT THE AUTHOR

Dr. Madeleine F. Wallace is a dynamic and versatile professional, author, serial entrepreneur, scientist, investor, and the founder of Windrose Vision. Originally from Peru, she immigrated to the US, excelled academically, and is among a select group of foreign-born Latinas in the U.S.—less than 1%—who hold a doctorate degree.

With over two decades of experience guiding and facilitating transformations across commercial, nonprofit, and governmental sectors, Dr. Wallace possesses a unique blend of strategic acumen and scientific expertise. This specialized skill set enables her to bridge interdisciplinary divides and transcend traditional field boundaries. She applies insights and lessons learned in one domain to solve challenges in another, fostering innovation and driving progress across a wide spectrum of fields in the public sector and businesses.

In the public sector, she was celebrated for her invaluable contributions to the National Institutes of Health (NIH), a world leader in funding biomedical and behavioral research. As Director of the Office of Evaluation and Performance, Dr. Wallace spearheaded efforts to bolster the NIH's ability to measure and showcase the impact of its research by strengthening their planning, monitoring, and evaluation activities.

She founded Windrose Vision, a consulting firm skilled in steering a vast range of projects across diverse industries, delivering strategic advice on scalability, sustainability, operational excellence, and data optimization. Equipped with proven methodologies, Windrose Vision, under the guidance of Dr. Wallace, excels in pinpointing the key shifts that propel revenue, slash costs, and streamline processes. In a world where digital transformation is a necessity, Windrose Vision emerges as a quintessential partner for government, non-profit, and commercial entities alike.

Dr. Wallace is adept at addressing existing challenges and developing innovative solutions. She developed the SEAM framework, a strategic tool

specifically designed to facilitate the digital transformation of small organizations, as most available tools are tailored for larger entities. Dr. Wallace has developed frameworks to assess organizational performance and customize evidence-based interventions for diverse populations. These have been critical in areas such as cardiovascular disease prevention education, and in implementing interventions that focus on the co-occurrence of HIV and mental illness, and/or substance use disorder (SUD), as well as in the treatment of individuals with HIV. Her commitment to empowering women is steadfast and enduring. Remaining an active consultant in both the governmental and private sectors, she works to increase the presence of underrepresented groups within STEM and biomedical fields. Additionally, Dr. Wallace has made monumental contributions to the realms of Diversity, Equity, and Inclusion (DEI). This dedication has led to evaluating the effectiveness of current DEI programs or initiatives.

Dr. Wallace earned her Ph.D. in Sociology from the University of Tennessee and is a prestigious alumna of the Latino Business Action Network (LBAN)'s Business Scaling program at Stanford University Graduate School of Business, the Goldman Sachs 10,000 Small Businesses' Entrepreneurship program at Babson College, and the National Hispana Leadership Institute (NHLI)'s Executive Leadership Program at the John F. Kennedy School of Government, Harvard University.

APPENDIX 1

Access all figures and blank
templates available at
https://www.madeleinewallace.com/#resources
or by scanning this QR code.